The Riverside Literature Series

THE NIGHT BEFORE THANKSGIVING
A WHITE HERON
AND SELECTED STORIES

BY

SARAH ORNE JEWETT

WITH INTRODUCTORY NOTES, AND QUESTIONS AND SUGGESTIONS

BY

KATHARINE H. SHUTE

HEAD OF THE DEPARTMENT OF ENGLISH IN THE
BOSTON NORMAL SCHOOL

BOSTON NEW YORK CHICAGO
HOUGHTON MIFFLIN COMPANY
The Riverside Press Cambridge

COPYRIGHT, 1877, BY JAMES R. OSGOOD & CO.

COPYRIGHT, 1883, 1886, 1889, 1893, 1895, 1899, AND 1905,
BY SARAH ORNE JEWETT

COPYRIGHT, 1911, BY HOUGHTON MIFFLIN COMPANY

COPYRIGHT, 1911 AND 1914, BY MARY R. JEWETT

ALL RIGHTS RESERVED

The Riverside Press
CAMBRIDGE . MASSACHUSETTS
U . S . A

In the interest of creating a more extensive selection of rare historical book reprints, we have chosen to reproduce this title even though it may possibly have occasional imperfections such as missing and blurred pages, missing text, poor pictures, markings, dark backgrounds and other reproduction issues beyond our control. Because this work is culturally important, we have made it available as a part of our commitment to protecting, preserving and promoting the world's literature. Thank you for your understanding.

CONTENTS

To the Teacher	iii
To the Pupil	ix
A White Heron	1
The Garden Tea	17
A Little Traveler	25
The Circus at Denby	34
The Night before Thanksgiving	45
A War Debt	53
Miss Esther's Guest	81
Martha's Lady	94

TO THE TEACHER

To encourage in boys and girls a taste for good reading and to give them some knowledge of where to turn to satisfy that taste is without any question one of the most beneficent things the schools can do. The introduction of literature within recent years into the common school curriculum has had this object primarily in view, but has too often failed of its accomplishment. So long as careful investigations of the reading of children reveal a gulf between the reading done in school and that done outside which at first sight seems impassable; and so long as the reading of the majority of adults who have been educated in the common schools continues to be second-rate at best, and often cheap and sensational, we cannot pride ourselves upon the success of our literary courses in their primary object.

This failure is due in many instances to the fact that the literature read in school is so far removed, both in subject matter and in form, from the things which a child chooses for himself, that the school-room procedures fail to make connection with the habits of out-of-school life. This school-room literature has consisted largely of a rather limited selection of standard English verse, of classics adapted to the understanding of children, and of children's stories. Now it need hardly be said that these things are all essential and desirable and that each has its place in a child's education. An acquaintance with English verse is an indispensable experience, one that should begin in the nursery and never be discontinued; an early introduction to the classics is invaluable; and children's stories help a child both to interpret and to enlarge his own life. But it is a rare boy or girl, man or woman whose voluntary reading will consist largely of standard verse or of any form of the classics, original or adapted; and it is certainly not desirable that boys and girls of high-grade grammar and high school age should keep on reading children's stories, as frequently does occur unless an even more regrettable thing happens, that is, the development of a taste, independently of school influence, for adult fiction of a second or third-rate quality. The natural human demand is for stories; and if a person has no liking for the better sort of story, he will read a worse sort, for stories of some sort he will have.

As in all matters of art, education of the taste in youth makes a difference for life. In the case of stories, the school has a priceless opportunity, — the opportunity to introduce boys and girls to people worth knowing, to standards worth having, and to a way of looking at the problems of life worth trusting. In the highest grade and in the high school, the great English novel should certainly have the established place which it is gradually making for itself; but there is another form of prose literature, now rarely used, which ought to yield permanent and valuable returns, namely, the short story, for the hurried habits of the age make the short story a peculiarly inviting literary form.

Now the short story — a literary type which our pupils will constantly meet in the magazines — may be of high literary grade or may be — to borrow an expression of Thackeray's — "extraordinary ordinary" in both substance and style. A taste for the better sort of short story cultivated in school would be a very practical contribution toward the resources of actual life; and a few well-chosen short stories read in school should serve as a means of developing simple canons of criticism that cannot fail to have a wholesome influence on later independent choices. In choosing stories for school use from among those that have an accepted literary standing, two tests may be applied: first, does the story contain characters and situations naturally pleasing to a young reader; second, does it contain standards and ideals good for him to meet? Or to modify the form of the questions: —

will a young reader find here what he desires; and will he find what we older people desire him to have? The story which meets one test but not the other, is distinctly not suited to our purpose.

New England has grown rich in short-story writers during the past thirty years. One of the best-beloved, Sarah Orne Jewett, has recently finished her work, leaving the world poorer because her gracious personality and rich gifts have been withdrawn from it; but the precious legacy of her stories remains. These are too genuine, too human, too full of the spirit of New England to be relegated to the shelves of mature and cultivated book-lovers only. A wider circle of readers should be found than that which has hailed with delight each new story as it came fresh from her pen. She has written many things which growing girls and boys care for, especially when they read them with some older friend who appreciates the insight, the sympathy, the delicate taste, the delicious humor, the perfect restraint which characterize them all. Only a few of these have been gathered together in this little volume, but others have been suggested in the introductory notes in the hope that the teacher will read some of them to the pupils and will encourage them to get others from the public libraries to read outside of school.

The short story has developed so distinctive a character and so finished a form since Poe's masterly analysis of it years ago, that by some critics it is as sharply differentiated from other prose forms as the sonnet is, for example, from other verse forms. The essential characteristics of the short story are first, brevity; second, a unity of purpose which forbids digressions; and third, a dominating emotion or atmosphere of feeling animating the writer and controlling the reader. It would be interesting to the teacher to read these stories of Miss Jewett's with these characteristics in mind, for they are written with such apparent unconsciousness that a hasty reading would fail to reveal the exquisite art with which they are constructed. Another interesting point of view from which the teacher might enjoy reading the stories, is that of the elements or materials of which they — in common with all narrative — are composed, — plot, background, characters. We have often in Miss Jewett's stories a very complete and well organized little plot, as in "A White Heron" and "Miss Esther's Guest." Perhaps the most unique bit of plot in her short stories is to be found in "The Only Rose," in which the solution of the whole vexing problem is as satisfactory as it is unexpected. But plot was very evidently not Miss Jewett's chief concern. It is in the delineation of character that she excels; and her handling of background is a close second to her treatment of character. Whether this background is a literal background of outdoor scenery and homely interiors or an atmosphere of customs and manners, the result is equally finished and convincing.

Miss Jewett was so perfect an artist that a shallow adherence to the doctrine of art for art's sake might lead one to conclude that she was never consciously a teacher. That she thought of herself as a teacher, however, is delightfully attested by the following passage from one of her letters, — "You must remember that a story-writer does not have her readers before her with their eager faces as a teacher (I was going to say, *the other kind of teacher*) does!" Since she thought of herself as another kind of teacher, we teachers may feel an especial pleasure in helping young readers to find and appropriate her message. This message of friendly faith in human nature I have suggested very simply in the pages addressed to the pupils; and it may be found again and again in the stories.

But the pupils' realization of this message will depend upon the teacher's good sense and sympathy and not upon analysis and didacticism. Her larger view, deeper insight, and more cultivated taste may often help a child to interpret and enjoy what would otherwise be beyond his reach. Let her by no means impose her estimates, her judgments, but let her rather encourage a free expression of opinion in regard to characters, situations, and motives, no matter how crude it may be, lending her riper experience, as she would in any other matter, to influence but not to determine the more youthful point of view.

The notes and questions accompanying these stories are intended as suggestions only. Each teacher who reads for herself will find other points which she will wish to make with her own pupils. It is hoped that the pupils will read with the teacher the pages entitled "To the Pupil," and the introductory note accompanying each story. The questions have been made human rather than technical, and the emphasis has been placed on those aspects of the story that contribute to the impression which we desire to have the pupil carry away from the reading. As a rule the most obvious questions have been omitted, except where they have a bearing upon this resulting impression. Many questions which may seem irrelevant are asked for the purpose of training the children to read less superficially than is their habit, and to take intelligent pleasure in the incidental touches and suggestiveness of the writer. The questions are placed at the end of the story in every case except "The Garden Tea," but the teacher may often find it desirable to write two or three of the questions on the board before the pupils read the story, to serve as a stimulus to thought and discussion while the story is being read. It is sometimes interesting to the pupils to answer one or more questions in writing, not as a means of examination, but as an incentive to independence of thought and opinion. It adds greatly to the interest if the answers are read aloud and discussed. Another interesting exercise is to permit the pupils to write questions of their own to be asked of their classmates and the teacher. And a never-failing source of interest is the selection of situations in the stories especially adapted to illustration, with some discussion of the essential features of the illustrations.

In work of this sort the teacher is often confronted by a

vexing but amusing problem, the problem of the child who "reads ahead" while the story is being read aloud. Out of order as he is, technically speaking, his behavior is more encouraging than that of the pupil who is cheerfully keeping his place, for he is genuinely interested. He is, indeed, giving incontestable proof of the very state of mind which we are trying to create. Two aids to the solution of the problem may be suggested: first, these stories are so little dependent upon plot for their chief interest that the pupils may be permitted, even encouraged, to read them at odd moments or to take them home; second, when they are being read orally, the teacher should frequently take her turn at the reading, especially in difficult passages and in passages where there is considerable dialect. Not only will the pleasure of the pupils be greatly increased by listening to the teacher's more intelligent and sympathetic interpretation, but their own reading will improve under the stimulus of the teacher's better reading. Unless wreck is to be made of the whole experiment of introducing stories of this sort into the schoolroom, it must never be lost sight of that the main purpose, the objective point, of the work is not to afford opportunity for oral reading to as many pupils as possible, but to interest the pupils genuinely and happily in these stories. Confusion of aims and the substitution of mere incidental aims for vital ones is the cause of much of the wasted time and energy which make even our earnest efforts unproductive.

When all is said, the one thing of importance is to help our boys and girls to *live* so genuinely in the story which they are reading, that their thought will turn back to it afterwards as to a real experience. Formal treatment will kill interest and will defeat the very purpose with which the stories have been gathered together and the questions written; but human fellowship with the people who move through these stories, and glimpses into the beauty of the outdoor world such as they afford, should make life richer not for the moment only, but for the years that are coming.

writing short stories and sketches for older people; there
are nearly one hundred of these, every one of them worth
reading, although they vary, of course, in merit and beauty.
Her most perfect book, her "high-water mark," is a series
of sketches bound together by a slight thread of narrative,
called "The Country of the Pointed Firs." If she had
written this only, New England would still have reason to
be proud and grateful.

Many of her short stories are not a bit too old for boys
and girls; and a few of these are gathered together in this
little volume. You will not find here tales of exciting adventure; but you will find people who seem as real as your own
neighbors, much kindliness, much humor, and wise ways of
looking at life. Another thing that you will find is a close
and loving observation of nature, as might be expected of a
person who speaks of "the country out of which I grew, and
where every bush and tree seem like my cousins." Scattered through her stories are stately, old-fashioned gardens,
such as the one described in "Martha's Lady"; bare New
England pastures with their mulleins and junipers and moss-
grown rocks; winding wood-roads and shaded village streets;
rocky bits of sea-coast; and wide green marshes where the
sea comes and goes. If you know and love these things
already, it will be a delight to you to see them through Miss
Jewett's eyes; if many of them are strange to you, begin
to be on the outlook for them, — life is a hundred times
as interesting when we are alive to the beauty that is all
about us.

Miss Jewett had a keen sense of humor and never failed to
recognize the laughable side of things; but her humor was
full of sympathy; she never made fun of people, never held
them up to ridicule. Read "Miss Esther's Guest" and see
how true this is; you don't find yourself laughing *at* dear
Miss Esther and quaint old Mr. Rill; you laugh — to be
sure — but with friendliness. But Miss Jewett recognized
not only the humorous aspect of New England life, but the

sadder side with all its privation and narrowness. In a very lovely chapter in "Betty Leicester" called "Up Country," we get a glimpse of two women, each living, solitary, in her lonely little house on the long hillside. Some writers would let you feel the loneliness only, and would leave you with no feeling for the women but pity; but Miss Jewett helps you to see their cheeriness and friendliness and strength. Now and then she paints a sordid and unlovely nature, narrow and even cruel in its selfishness, as in "A Landless Farmer," "In Dark New England Days," and "The Failure of David Berry." As has been said, she was not blind to the more worthless, degenerate side of New England life, as we find in reading such stories as "The Courting of Sister Wisby" and "Miss Debby's Neighbors." A truthful writer could not ignore these things; but she never lets us feel for one moment that the world is made up of such people. She emphasizes, rather, the hopefulness and promise of human life.

One very interesting feature of Miss Jewett's stories is her use of dialect. She was evidently an unusually close observer of speech; she noticed not only the odd ways in which people pronounce words, but the characteristic words and phrases which they use. In reporting conversation, however, she does not weary the reader, as many writers do, with an excessive use of dialect, but records enough only to give a true impression of the person's habit of speech. The intrusion of a rather ambitious word into the midst of otherwise uneducated speech is very characteristic of the New Englander, and this Miss Jewett illustrates again and again. You will notice it with pleasure in reading "Miss Esther's Guest."

There are two reasons why you young people should get in the way of reading the best books while you are young. In the first place they provide you with companionship of the right sort now; and in the second place they help to give you a standard of what is worth reading that will be a guide to you all your lives. That Miss Jewett's work is among these best things there can be no question. You will be interested to hear what James Russell Lowell once said of it: " Nothing more pleasingly characteristic of rural life in New England has been written than that from the pen of Miss Sarah Orne Jewett."

During the last fifty years an astonishing number of really excellent short stories have been written in the United States. Probably nothing else has done more to make people belonging to all parts of the country — East and West, North and South — acquainted with one another's lives and ways of looking at things than these short stories. You will readily see that in a country like ours, so extended in its territory and made up of so many different kinds of people, one of the most necessary things is that we should know and understand one another, for our great Union cannot grow in unity of spirit if the people living in different sections of the country misunderstand and distrust one another. The local short story, then, has a use beyond that of entertaining and refreshing its readers; it is a means of bringing the people of the nation nearer together.

Many writers — men and women — share the honor of interpreting the people of this great land to one another. You will wish to read much that they have written; and if you are the right sort of reader you will be wiser and broader-minded for the reading. But you cannot do better than to begin your acquaintance with these short-story writers by reading one who was so true and loving a student of nature and of human life, so perfect an artist in her mode of telling what she saw and heard, so wise a guide in the "fine art of living" as Sarah Orne Jewett.

A WHITE HERON

The story of "A White Heron" is to be found in one of Miss Jewett's earlier collections, called *A White Heron, and Other Stories*. Other delightful stories in the same volume are "Mary and Martha" and "A Business Man."

"A White Heron" has been more widely read, perhaps, than any other of Miss Jewett's short stories, and is loved by both old people and young people. It is what we call "a classic," that is, a bit of literature so perfect of its kind that it is likely to live for many years.

I

THE woods were already filled with shadows one June evening, just before eight o'clock, though a bright sunset still glimmered faintly among the trunks of the trees. A little girl was driving home her cow, a plodding, dilatory, provoking creature in her behavior, but a valued companion for all that. They were going away from whatever light there was, and striking deep into the woods; but their feet were familiar with the path, and it was no matter whether their eyes could see it or not.

There was hardly a night the summer through when the old cow could be found waiting at the pasture bars; on the contrary, it was her greatest pleasure to hide herself away among the huckleberry bushes, and though she wore a loud bell she had made the discovery that if one stood perfectly still it would not ring. So Sylvia had to hunt for her until she found her, and call Co'! Co'! with never an answering Moo, until her childish patience was quite spent. If the creature had not given good milk and plenty of it, the case would have seemed very different to her owners. Besides, Sylvia had all the time there was, and very little use to make of it. Sometimes in pleasant weather it was a consolation to look upon the cow's pranks as an intelligent attempt to play hide and seek, and as the child had no playmates she lent herself to this amusement with a good deal of zest. Though this chase had been so long that the wary animal herself had given an unusual signal of her whereabouts, Sylvia had only laughed when she came upon Mistress Moolly at the swamp-side, and urged her affectionately homeward with a twig of birch leaves. The old cow was not inclined to wander farther, she even turned in the right direction for once as they left the pasture, and stepped along the road at a good pace. She was quite ready to be milked now, and seldom stopped to browse. Sylvia wondered what her grandmother would say because they were so late. It was a great while since she had left home at half-past five o'clock, but everybody knew the difficulty of making this errand a short one. Mrs. Tilley had chased the hornéd torment too many summer evenings herself to blame any one else for lingering, and was only thankful as she waited that she had Sylvia, nowadays, to give such valuable assistance. The good woman suspected that Sylvia loitered occasionally on her own account; there never was such a child for straying about out-of-doors since the world was made! Everybody said that it was a good change for a little maid who had tried to grow for eight years in a crowded manufacturing town, but, as for Sylvia herself, it seemed as if she never had been alive at all before she came to live at the farm. She thought often with wistful compassion of a wretched geranium that belonged to a town neighbor.

"'Afraid of folks,'" old Mrs. Tilley said to herself, with a smile, after she had made the unlikely choice of Sylvia from her daughter's houseful of children, and was returning to the farm. "'Afraid of folks,' they said! I guess she won't be troubled no great with 'em up to the old place!" When they reached the door of the lonely house and stopped to unlock it, and the cat came to purr loudly, and rub against them, a deserted pussy, indeed, but fat with young robins, Sylvia whispered that this was a beautiful place to live in, and she never should wish to go home.

The companions followed the shady woodroad, the cow taking slow steps and the child very fast ones. The cow stopped long at the brook to drink, as if the pasture were not half a swamp, and Sylvia stood still and waited, letting her bare feet cool themselves in the shoal water, while the great twilight moths struck softly against her. She waded on through the brook as the cow moved away, and listened to the thrushes with a heart that beat fast with pleasure. There was a stirring in the great boughs overhead. They were full of little birds and beasts that seemed to be wide awake, and going about their world, or else saying good-night to each other in sleepy twitters. Sylvia herself felt sleepy as she walked along. However, it was not much farther to the house, and the air was soft and sweet. She was not often in the woods so late as this, and it made her feel as if she were a part of the gray shadows and the moving leaves. She was just thinking how long it seemed since she first came to the farm a year ago, and wondering if everything went on in the noisy town just the same as when she was there; the thought of the great red-faced boy who used to chase and frighten her made her hurry along the path to escape from the shadow of the trees.

Suddenly this little woods-girl is horror-stricken to hear a clear whistle not very far away. Not a bird's whistle, which would have a sort of friendliness, but a boy's whistle, determined, and somewhat aggressive. Sylvia left the cow to whatever sad fate might await her, and stepped discreetly aside into the bushes, but she was just too late. The enemy had discovered her, and called out in a very cheerful and persuasive tone, "Halloa, little girl, how far is it to the road?" and trembling Sylvia answered almost inaudibly, "A good ways."

She did not dare to look boldly at the tall young man, who carried a gun over his shoulder, but she came out of her bush and again followed the cow, while he walked alongside.

"I have been hunting for some birds," the stranger said kindly, "and I have lost my way, and need a friend very much. Don't be afraid," he added gallantly. "Speak up and tell me what your name is, and whether you think I can spend the night at your house, and go out gunning early in the morning."

Sylvia was more alarmed than before. Would not her grandmother consider her much to blame? But who could have foreseen such an accident as this? It did not seem to be her fault, and she hung her head as if the stem of it were broken, but managed to answer "Sylvy," with much effort when her companion again asked her name.

Mrs. Tilley was standing in the doorway when the trio came into view. The cow gave a loud moo by way of explanation.

"Yes, you'd better speak up for yourself, you old trial! Where'd she tucked herself away this time, Sylvy?" But Sylvia kept an awed silence; she knew by instinct that her grandmother did not comprehend the gravity of the situation. She must be mistaking the stranger for one of the farmer-lads of the region.

The young man stood his gun beside the door, and dropped a lumpy game-bag beside it; then he bade Mrs. Tilley good-evening, and repeated his wayfarer's story, and asked if he could have a night's lodging.

"Put me anywhere you like," he said. "I must be off early in the morning, before day; but I am very hungry, indeed. You can give me some milk at any rate, that's plain."

"Dear sakes, yes," responded the hostess, whose long slumbering hospitality seemed to be easily awakened. "You might fare better if you went out to the main road a mile or so, but you're welcome to what we've got. I'll milk right off, and you make yourself at home. You can sleep on husks or feathers," she proffered graciously. "I raised them all myself. There's good pasturing for geese just below here towards the ma'sh. Now step round and set a plate for the gentleman, Sylvy!" And Sylvia promptly stepped. She was glad to have something to do, and she was hungry herself.

It was a surprise to find so clean and comfortable a little dwelling in this New England wilderness. The young man had known the horrors of its most primitive housekeeping, and the dreary squalor of that level of society which does not rebel at the companionship of hens. This was the best thrift of an old-fashioned farmstead, though on such a small scale that it seemed like a hermitage. He listened eagerly to the old woman's quaint talk, he watched Sylvia's pale face and shining gray eyes with ever growing enthusiasm, and insisted that this was the best supper he had eaten for a month, and afterward the new-made friends sat down in the door-way together while the moon came up.

Soon it would be berry-time, and Sylvia was a great help at picking. The cow was a good milker, though a plaguy thing to keep track of, the hostess gossiped frankly, adding presently that she had buried four children, so Sylvia's mother, and a son (who might be dead) in California were all the children she had left. "Dan, my boy, was a great hand to go gunning," she explained sadly. "I never wanted for pa'tridges or gray squer'ls while he was to home. He's been a great wand'rer, I expect, and he's no hand to write letters. There, I don't blame him, I'd ha' seen the world myself if it had been so I could."

"Sylvy takes after him," the grandmother continued affectionately, after a minute's pause. "There ain't a foot o' ground she don't know her way over, and the wild creaturs counts her one o' themselves. Squer'ls she'll tame to come an' feed right out o' her hands, and all sorts o' birds. Last winter she got the jay-birds to bangeing here, and I believe she'd 'a' scanted herself of her own meals to have plenty to throw out amongst 'em, if I had n't kep' watch. Anything but crows, I tell her, I'm willin' to help support — though Dan he had a tamed one o' them that did seem to have reason same as folks. It was round here a good spell after he went away. Dan an' his father they did n't hitch, — but he never held up his head ag'in after Dan had dared him an' gone off."

The guest did not notice this hint of family sorrows in his eager interest in something else.

"So Sylvy knows all about birds, does she?" he ex-

claimed, as he looked round at the little girl who sat,
very demure but increasingly sleepy, in the moonlight.
"I am making a collection of birds myself. I have been
at it ever since I was a boy." (Mrs. Tilley smiled.)
"There are two or three very rare ones I have been
hunting for these five years. I mean to get them on
my own ground if they can be found."

"Do you cage 'em up?" asked Mrs. Tilley doubtfully, in response to this enthusiastic announcement.

"Oh no, they're stuffed and preserved, dozens and
dozens of them," said the ornithologist, "and I have
shot or snared every one myself. I caught a glimpse
of a white heron a few miles from here on Saturday,
and I have followed it in this direction. They have never
been found in this district at all. The little white
heron, it is," and he turned again to look at Sylvia
with the hope of discovering that the rare bird was
one of her acquaintances.

But Sylvia was watching a hop-toad in the narrow
footpath.

"You would know the heron if you saw it," the
stranger continued eagerly. "A queer tall white bird
with soft feathers and long thin legs. And it would
have a nest perhaps in the top of a high tree, made of
sticks, something like a hawk's nest."

Sylvia's heart gave a wild beat; she knew that
strange white bird, and had once stolen softly near
where it stood in some bright green swamp grass, away
over at the other side of the woods. There was an open
place where the sunshine always seemed strangely yellow and hot, where tall, nodding rushes grew, and her
grandmother had warned her that she might sink in
the soft black mud underneath and never be heard of
more. Not far beyond were the salt marshes just this

side the sea itself, which Sylvia wondered and dreamed much about, but never had seen, whose great voice could sometimes be heard above the noise of the woods on stormy nights.

"I can't think of anything I should like so much as to find that heron's nest," the handsome stranger was saying. "I would give ten dollars to anybody who could show it to me," he added desperately, "and I mean to spend my whole vacation hunting for it if need be. Perhaps it was only migrating, or had been chased out of its own region by some bird of prey."

Mrs. Tilley gave amazed attention to all this, but Sylvia still watched the toad, not divining, as she might have done at some calmer time, that the creature wished to get to its hole under the doorstep, and was much hindered by the unusual spectators at that hour of the evening. No amount of thought, that night, could decide how many wished-for treasures the ten dollars, so lightly spoken of, would buy.

The next day the young sportsman hovered about the woods, and Sylvia kept him company, having lost her first fear of the friendly lad, who proved to be most kind and sympathetic. He told her many things about the birds and what they knew and where they lived and what they did with themselves. And he gave her a jack-knife, which she thought as great a treasure as if she were a desert-islander. All day long he did not once make her troubled or afraid except when he brought down some unsuspecting singing creature from its bough. Sylvia would have liked him vastly better without his gun; she could not understand why he killed the very birds he seemed to like so much. But as the day waned, Sylvia still watched the young man with loving admiration. She had never seen anybody so charming and delightful; the woman's heart, asleep in the child, was vaguely thrilled by a dream of love. Some premonition of that great power stirred and swayed these young creatures who traversed the solemn woodlands with soft-footed silent care. They stopped to listen to a bird's song; they pressed forward again eagerly, parting the branches — speaking to each other rarely and in whispers; the young man going first and Sylvia following, fascinated, a few steps behind, with her gray eyes dark with excitement.

She grieved because the longed-for white heron was elusive, but she did not lead the guest, she only followed, and there was no such thing as speaking first. The sound of her own unquestioned voice would have terrified her — it was hard enough to answer yes or no when there was need of that. At last evening began to fall, and they drove the cow home together, and Sylvia smiled with pleasure when they came to the place where she heard the whistle and was afraid only the night before.

II

Half a mile from home, at the farther edge of the woods, where the land was highest, a great pine-tree stood, the last of its generation. Whether it was left for a boundary mark, or for what reason, no one could say; the woodchoppers who had felled its mates were dead and gone long ago, and a whole forest of sturdy trees, pines and oaks and maples, had grown again. But the stately head of this old pine towered above them all and made a landmark for sea and shore miles and miles away. Sylvia knew it well. She had always believed that whoever climbed to the top of it could see the ocean; and the little girl had often laid her hand on the great rough trunk and looked up wistfully at those dark boughs that the wind always stirred, no matter how hot and still the air might be below. Now she thought of the tree with a new excitement, for why, if one climbed it at break of day, could not one see all the world, and easily discover from whence the white heron flew, and mark the place, and find the hidden nest?

What a spirit of adventure, what wild ambition! What fancied triumph and delight and glory for the later morning when she could make known the secret! It was almost too real and too great for the childish heart to bear.

All night the door of the little house stood open and the whippoorwills came and sang upon the very step. The young sportsman and his old hostess were sound asleep, but Sylvia's great design kept her broad awake and watching. She forgot to think of sleep. The short summer night seemed as long as the winter darkness, and at last when the whippoorwills ceased, and she was afraid the morning would after all come too soon, she stole out of the house and followed the pasture path through the woods, hastening toward the open ground beyond, listening with a sense of comfort and companionship to the drowsy twitter of a half-awakened bird, whose perch she had jarred in passing. Alas, if the great wave of human interest which flooded for the first time this dull little life should sweep away the satisfactions of an existence heart to heart with nature and the dumb life of the forest!

There was the huge tree asleep yet in the paling moonlight, and small and silly Sylvia began with utmost bravery to mount to the top of it, with tingling, eager blood coursing the channels of her whole frame, with her bare feet and fingers, that pinched and held like bird's claws to the monstrous ladder reaching up, up, almost to the sky itself. First she must mount the white-oak tree that grew alongside, where she was almost lost among the dark branches and the green leaves heavy and wet with dew; a bird fluttered off its nest, and a red squirrel ran to and fro and scolded pettishly at the harmless housebreaker. Sylvia felt her way easily. She had often climbed there, and knew that higher still one of the oak's upper branches chafed against the pine trunk, just where its lower boughs were set close together. There, when she made the dangerous pass from one tree to the other, the great enterprise would really begin.

She crept out along the swaying oak limb at last, and took the daring step across into the old pine-tree. The way was harder than she thought; she must reach far and hold fast, the sharp dry twigs caught and held her and scratched her like angry talons, the pitch made her thin little fingers clumsy and stiff as she went round and round the tree's great stem, higher and higher upward. The sparrows and robins in the woods below were beginning to wake and twitter to the dawn, yet it seemed much lighter there aloft in the pine-tree, and the child knew she must hurry if her project were to be of any use.

The tree seemed to lengthen itself out as she went up, and to reach farther and farther upward. It was like a great main-mast to the voyaging earth; it must truly have been amazed that morning through all its ponderous frame as it felt this determined spark of human spirit wending its way from higher branch to branch. Who knows how steadily the least twigs held themselves to advantage this light, weak creature on her way! The old pine must have loved his new dependent. More than all the hawks, and bats, and moths, and even the sweet-voiced thrushes, was the brave, beating heart of the solitary gray-eyed child. And the tree stood still and frowned away the winds that June morning while the dawn grew bright in the east.

Sylvia's face was like a pale star, if one had seen it from the ground, when the last thorny bough was past, and she stood trembling and tired but wholly triumphant, high in the tree-top. Yes, there was the sea with the dawning sun making a golden dazzle over it, and toward that glorious east flew two hawks with slow-moving pinions. How low they looked in the air from that height when one had only seen them before far up, and dark against the blue sky. Their gray feathers were as soft as moths; they seemed only a little way from the tree, and Sylvia felt as if she too could go flying away among the clouds. Westward, the woodlands and farms reached miles and miles into the distance; here and there were church steeples, and white villages, truly it was a vast and awesome world!

The birds sang louder and louder. At last the sun came up bewilderingly bright. Sylvia could see the white sails of ships out at sea, and the clouds that were purple and rose-colored and yellow at first began to fade away. Where was the white heron's nest in the sea of green branches, and was this wonderful sight and pageant of the world the only reward for having climbed to such a giddy height? Now look down again, Sylvia, where the green marsh is set among the shining birches and dark hemlocks; there where you saw the white heron once you will see him again; look, look! a white spot of him like a single floating feather comes up from the dead hemlock and grows larger, and rises, and comes close at last, and goes by the landmark pine with steady sweep of wing and outstretched slender neck and crested head. And wait! wait! do not move a foot or a finger, little girl, do not send an arrow of light and consciousness from your two eager eyes, for the heron has perched on a pine bough not far beyond yours, and cries back to his mate on the nest and plumes his feathers for the new day!

The child gives a long sigh a minute later when a company of shouting cat-birds comes also to the tree, and vexed by their fluttering and lawlessness the solemn heron goes away. She knows his secret now, the wild, light, slender bird that floats and wavers, and goes back like an arrow presently to his home in the green world beneath. Then Sylvia, well satisfied, makes her perilous way down again, not daring to look far below the branch she stands on, ready to cry sometimes because her fingers ache and her lamed feet slip; wondering over and over again what the stranger would say to her, and what he would think when she told him how to find his way straight to the heron's nest.

"Sylvy, Sylvy!" called the busy old grandmother again and again, but nobody answered, and the small husk bed was empty and Sylvia had disappeared.

The guest waked from a dream, and remembering his day's pleasure hurried to dress himself that it might sooner begin. He was sure from the way the shy little girl looked once or twice yesterday that she had at least seen the white heron, and now she must really be made to tell. Here she comes now, paler than ever, and her worn old frock is torn and tattered, and smeared with pine pitch. The grandmother and the sportsman stand in the door together and question her, and the splendid moment has come to speak of the dead hemlock-tree by the green marsh.

But Sylvia does not speak after all, though the old grandmother fretfully rebukes her, and the young man's kind, appealing eyes are looking straight in her own. He can make them rich with money; he has promised it, and they are poor now. He is so well worth making happy, and he waits to hear the story she can tell.

No, she must keep silence! What is it that suddenly forbids her and makes her dumb? Has she been nine years growing and now, when the great world for the first time puts out a hand to her, must she thrust it aside for a bird's sake? The murmur of the pine's green branches is in her ears, she remembers how the white heron came flying through the golden air and how they watched the sea and the morning together, and Sylvia cannot speak; she cannot tell the heron's secret and give its life away.

Dear loyalty, that suffered a sharp pang as the guest went away disappointed later in the day, that could have served and followed him and loved him as a dog loves! Many a night Sylvia heard the echo of his whistle haunting the pasture path as she came home with the loitering cow. She forgot even her sorrow at the sharp report of his gun and the sight of thrushes and sparrows dropping silent to the ground, their songs hushed and their pretty feathers stained and wet with blood. Were the birds better friends than their hunter might have been, — who can tell? Whatever treasures were lost to her, woodlands and summer-time, remember! Bring your gifts and graces and tell your secrets to this lonely country child!

QUESTIONS AND SUGGESTIONS

1. How many years had Sylvia lived in the manufacturing town?
2. How did she feel on arriving at her grandmother's house?
3. How old was she when the story opens?
4. Tell how the house appeared inside.
5. What did the house stand near?
6. Where was the pasture?
7. What could sometimes be heard, louder than the wind, beyond the near-by woods?
8. What does Miss Jewett tell us which shows how remote and safe the little house was?
9. Describe Sylvia's looks.
10. What proof does the story give that Sylvia was "afraid of folks," as her mother had said?
11. What was Sylvia's nearest approach to a game with playmates?
12. What is the first suggestion that Sylvia was especially interested in birds?
13. Name as many as you can from memory of the birds mentioned in the story. Which of these have you ever seen or heard?
14. The reference to the hop-toad and the red squirrel shows Miss Jewett's acquaintance with the habits of these little creatures. Recall what she tells about them. Do you know anything else about them?
15. Without really describing the grandmother, Miss Jewett makes us feel acquainted with her. Tell some of the things you know about her.

16. What was it in the stranger that made him so likable?

17. Why did Mrs. Tilley smile when the stranger said that he had been collecting birds ever since he was a boy?

18. "Sylvia would have liked him vastly better without his gun." Why? In recent years a great change has come in the way of studying wild creatures: the opera glass and the camera have partially taken the place of the gun. What can one learn by means of these harmless weapons that cannot be learned with the gun?

19. Give two reasons for Sylvia's wishing to find the nest for the stranger? Which do you think was the stronger?

20. How could the little girl find her way before sunrise?

21. Describe Sylvia's climb up the tree, from the tree's standpoint.

22. Tell all that Sylvia saw from the top of the great pine.

23. As she was coming down the tree, did she intend to tell the stranger about the nest?

24. Did you expect that she would tell him?

25. Why did she change her mind?

26. Was it easy for her to refuse to tell?

27. Find and read the words in which Sylvia's grandmother describes the little girl's fondness for wild creatures. Do you wonder that Sylvia could not betray such a trust!

THE GARDEN TEA

"The Garden Tea" is a chapter from *Betty Leicester*, a charming book for girls. Betty, who is about fifteen, has no mother; and her father, with whom Betty is on terms of most delightful good comradeship and whose companion she has been on many journeys, has gone to Alaska for the summer on a scientific expedition, sending Betty to Tideshead, a New England village, to spend the summer with his two aunts, Betty's great-aunts.

After you have read this chapter, you may enjoy discussing the following questions: —

1. In another chapter, Miss Jewett says of Betty and her father, "Their friends thought them good-looking, but it ought to be revealed in this story just what sort of good looks they had, since character makes the expression of people's faces." Tell what you think about Betty's looks after reading this chapter, and give your reasons.

2. In a letter to her father Betty once said of the Tideshead girls, "They think of every reason why you can't do things that you can do." What illustrations of that spirit do you find in this chapter?

3. Give two or three reasons why you would like Miss Barbara for an aunt.

THERE was a gnarled old pear-tree of great age and size that grew near Betty Leicester's east window. By leaning out a little she could touch the nearest bough. Aunt Barbara and Aunt Mary said that it was a most beautiful thing to see it in bloom in the spring; and the family cats were fond of climbing up and leaping across to the window-sill, while there were usually some birds perching in it when the coast was clear of pussies.

One day Betty was looking over from Mary Beck's and saw that the east window and the pear-tree branch were in plain sight; so the two girls invented a system of signals: one white handkerchief meant *come over*, and two meant *no*, but a single one in answer was for *yes*. A yellow handkerchief on the bough proposed a walk; and so the code went on, and was found capable of imparting much secret information. Sometimes the exchange of these signals took a far longer time than it did to run across from house to house, and at any rate in the first fortnight Mary and Betty spent the greater part of their waking hours together. Still the signal service, as they proudly called it, was of great use.

One morning, when Mary had been summoned, Betty came rushing to meet her.

"Aunt Barbara is going to let me have a tea-party. What do you think of that?" she cried.

Mary Beck looked pleased, and then a doubting look crept over her face.

"I don't know any of the boys and girls very well except you," Betty explained, "and Aunt Barbara likes the idea of having them come. Aunt Mary thinks that she can't come down, for the excitement would be too much for her, but I am going to tease her again as soon as I have time. It is to be a summer-house tea at six o'clock; it is lovely in the garden then. Just as soon as I have helped Serena a little longer, you and I will go to invite everybody. Serena is letting me beat eggs."

It was a great astonishment that Betty should take the serious occasion so lightly. Mary Beck would have planned it at least a week beforehand, and have worried and worked and been in despair; but here was Betty as gay as possible, and as for Aunt Barbara and Serena and Letty, they were gay too. It was entirely mysterious.

"I have sent word by Jonathan to the Picknell girls; he had an errand on that road. They looked so old and scared in church last Sunday that I kept thinking that they ought to have a good time. They don't come in to the village much, do they?" inquired Betty with great interest.

"Hardly ever, except Sundays," answered Mary Beck. "They turn red if you only look at them, but they are always talking together when they go by. One of them can draw beautifully. Oh, of course I go to school with them, but I don't know them very well."

"I hope they'll come, don't you?" said Betty, whisking away at the eggs. "I don't know when I've ever been where I could have a little party. I can have two or three girls to luncheon or tea almost any time, especially in London, but that's different. Who else now, Becky? Let's see if we choose the same ones."

"Mary and Julia Picknell, and Mary and Ellen Grant, and Lizzie French, and George Max, and Frank Crane, and my cousin Jim Beck, — Dan's too little. They would be eight, and you and I make ten — oh, that's too many!"

"Dear me, no!" said Betty lightly. "I thought of the Fosters, too" —

"We don't have much to do with the Fosters," said Mary Beck. "I don't see why that Nelly Foster started up and came to see you. I never go inside her house now. Everybody despises her father" —

"I think that Nelly is a dear-looking girl," insisted Betty. "I like her ever so much."

"They acted so stuck-up after Mr. Foster was put in jail," Mary went on. "People pitied them at first and were carrying about a subscription-paper, but Mrs. Foster wouldn't take anything, and said that they were going to support themselves. People don't like Mrs. Foster very well."

"Aunt Barbara respects her very much. She says that few women would show the courage she has shown. Perhaps she hasn't a nice way of speaking, but Aunt Barbara said that I must ask Harry and Nelly, when we were talking about to-night." Betty could not help a tone of triumph; she and Becky had fought a little about the Fosters before this.

"Harry is just like a wild Indian," said Mary Beck; "he goes fishing and trapping almost all the time. He won't know what to do at a party. I believe he makes ever so much money with his fish, and pays bills with it." Becky relented a little now. "Oh, dear, I haven't anything nice enough to wear," she added suddenly. "We never have parties in Tideshead, except at the vestry in the winter; and they're so poky."

"Oh, wear anything; it's going to be hot, that's all," said industrious Betty, in her business-like checked apron; and it now first dawned upon Becky's honest mind that it was not worth while to make one's self utterly miserable about one's clothes.

The two girls went scurrying away like squirrels presently to invite the guests. Nelly Foster looked delighted at the thought of such a pleasure.

"But I don't know what Harry will say," she added, doubtfully.

"Please ask him to be sure to come," urged Betty. "I should be so disappointed, and Aunt Barbara asked me to say that she depended upon him, for she knows him better than she does almost any of the young people." Nelly looked radiant at this, but Mary Beck was much offended. "I go to your Aunt Barbara's oftener than anybody," she said jealously, as they came away.

"She asked me to say that, and I did," maintained Betty. "Don't be cross, Becky, it's going to be such a jolly tea-party. Why, here's Jonathan back again already. Oh, good! the Picknells are happy to come."

The rest of the guests were quickly made sure of, and Betty and reluctant Mary went back to the house. It made Betty a little disheartened to find that her friend took every proposition on the wrong side; she seemed to think most things about a tea-party were impossible, and that all were difficult, and she saw lions in the way at every turn. It struck Betty, who was used to taking social events easily, that there was no pleasuring at all in the old village, though people were always saying how gay and delightful it *used* to be and how many guests *used* to come to town in the summer.

The old Leicester garden was a lovely place on a summer evening. Aunt Barbara had been surprised when Betty insisted that she wished to have supper there instead of in the dining-room; but Betty had known too many out-of-door feasts in foreign countries not to remember how charming they were and how small any dining-room seems in summer by contrast. And after a few minutes' thought, Aunt Barbara, too, who had been in France long before, asked Serena and Letty to spread the table under the large cherry-tree near the arbor; and there it stood presently, with its white cloth, and pink roses in two china bowls, all ready for the sandwiches and bread and butter and strawberries and sponge-cake, and chocolate to drink out of the prettiest cups in Tideshead. It was all simple and gay and charming, the little feast; and full of grievous self-consciousness as the shyest guest might have been when first met by Betty at the doorstep, the pleasure of the party itself proved most contagious, and all fears were forgotten. Everybody met on common ground for once, without any thought of self. It came with surprise to more than one girl's mind that a party was really so little trouble. It was such a pity that somebody did not have one every week.

Aunt Barbara was very good to Harry Foster, who seemed at first much older and soberer than the rest; but Betty demanded his services when she was going to pass the sandwiches again, and Letty had gone to the house for another pot of chocolate. "I will take the bread and butter; won't you please pass these?" she said. And away they went to the rest of the company, who were scattered along the arbor benches by twos and threes.

"I saw you in your boat when I first came up the river," Betty found time to say. "I did n't know who you were then, though I was sure you were one of the boys whom I used to play with. Some time when Nelly is going down could n't you take me too? I can row."

"Nelly would go if you would. I never thought to ask her. I always wish there were somebody else to see how pleasant it is" — and then a voice interrupted to ask what Harry was catching now.

"Bass," said Harry, with brightening face. "I do so well that I am sending them down to Riverport

every day that the packet goes, and I wish that I had
somebody to help me. You don't know what a rich old
river it is!"

"Why, if here is n't Aunt Mary!" cried Betty.
Sure enough, the eager voices and the laughter had
attracted another guest. And Aunt Barbara sprang
up joyfully and called for a shawl and footstool from
the house; but Betty did n't wait for them, and brought
Aunt Mary to the arbor bench. Nobody knew when
the poor lady had been in her own garden before, but
here she was at last, and had her supper with the rest.
The good doctor would have been delighted enough if
he had seen the sight.

Nothing had ever tasted so good as that out-of-door
supper. The white June moon came up, and its bright
light made the day longer; and when everybody had
eaten a last piece of sponge-cake, and the heap of strawberries on a great round Indian dish had been leveled,
what should be heard but sounds of a violin. Betty
had discovered that Seth Pond, — the clumsy, good-
natured Seth of all people! — had, as he said, "ears
for music," and had taught himself to play.

So they had a country-dance on the green, girls and
boys and Aunt Barbara, who had been a famous dancer
in her youth; and those who did n't know the steps of
"Money Musk" and the Virginia reel were put in the
middle of the line, and had plenty of time to learn before their turns came. Afterward Seth played "Bonny
Doon," and "Nelly was a Lady," and "Johnny Comes
Marching Home," and "Annie Laurie," and half a
dozen other songs, and everybody sang, but, to Betty's
delight, Mary Beck's voice led all the rest.

The moon was high in the sky when the guests went
away. It seemed like a new world to some young folks

who were there, and everybody was surprised because everybody else looked so pretty and was so surprisingly gay. Yet, here it was, the same old Tideshead after all!

"Aunt Barbara," said Betty, as that aunt sat on the side of Betty's four-post bed, — "Aunt Barbara, don't say good-night just yet. I must talk about one or two things before I forget them in the morning. Mary Picknell asked me ever so many questions about some of the pictures, but she knows more about them than I do, and I thought I would ask her to come some day so that you could tell her everything. She ought to be an artist. Did n't you see how she kept looking at the pictures? And then Harry Foster knows a lovely place down the river for a picnic, and can borrow boats enough beside his own to take us all there, only it's a secret yet. Harry said that it was a beautiful point of land, with large trees, and that there was a lane that came across the fields from the road, so that you could be driven down to meet us, if you disliked the boats."

"I am very fond of going on the water," said Aunt Barbara, with great spirit. "I knew that point, and those oak-trees, long before either of you was born. It was very polite of Harry to think of my coming with the young folks. Yes, we'll think about the picnic, certainly, but you must go to sleep now, Betty."

"Aunt Barbara must have been such a nice girl," thinks Betty, as the door shuts. "And if we go, Harry must take her in his boat. It is strange that Mary Beck should not like the Fosters, just because their father was a scamp."

But the room was still and dark, and sleepiness got the better of Betty's thoughts that night.

A LITTLE TRAVELER

"A Little Traveler" is one of the stories in a collection entitled *The Mate of the Daylight, and Friends Ashore.* You would be very much interested in two stories of New England country people contained in this volume, "A Landless Farmer" and "An Only Son."

THE day I met this little friend of mine (whom I never shall forget) I had just left some other friends, and I was sorry that my pleasant visit to them was over. I had a long journey to take before I reached home, and I was to take it alone. I did not mind this, in one way, for I had grown used to traveling by myself. I was lucky in having a most comfortable section in the sleeping-car, and I was well provided with books and lunch and pleasant thoughts. So, after I had looked out of the window for half an hour, I began to settle myself comfortably for the day or two I must spend in the train. There were several passengers, but no one whom I had ever seen before, and it was some time before I lost the feeling that I was with a company of unknown people, and began to take an interest in my fellow travelers separately. There was the usual young couple in very new clothes who tried to make us believe that they had been married these ten years, and there were two comfortable elderly women who knew each other and were journeying together, loudly talking over parish and neighborhood matters by the way. Not far from me was a round, red-cheeked old lady in a somewhat fantastic dress, with a big bonnet all covered with ends of narrow ribbon and lustreless bugles. I am sure she had made it herself and was proud and conscious of it. She had a great deal of small luggage in the compartment with her, and I thought she must be changing her home, for she never could be taking away so many and such curious-looking packages just for a visit. Besides these people there were four or five business men and a Catholic priest, and just opposite my own place was a little girl.

For some time I supposed she must belong to some one in the car, and had chosen to sit by herself for a while and look out of the window. Then I thought her father must have left her to go to some other part of the train where he had found some one to talk with. But two hours went by, and it was toward noon, and I watched the little thing grow sleepy and at last put her head down on the seat, and the doll she had held so carefully slid to the floor. I picked it up and put it on her arm again so she might find it when she waked. I had noticed that the conductor had spoken to her and I thought I would ask him about her when he next came by.

She did not sleep very long; the stopping of the train startled her, and when she opened her eyes I smiled at her and beckoned her to come to me. So she climbed the seat beside me, still holding the doll, and I asked her what its name was, and if she were all alone, and where she was going. She looked up gravely into my face and told me the doll's name and her own, and then she did not say anything more. She was younger than I had thought at first, and yet she was grave and sober and saddened. "Is n't your papa with you?" said I, but she only shook her head and looked up at me again as she sat beside me. I was strangely drawn to the little thing, — she puzzled me, and she was so wistful. She seemed contented, and we both looked out of the window, and talked now and then about the things we saw. She sat in my lap so she could see better.

After some time she said to me, "Mother is dead," in a half-questioning way, as if she expected me to say something; but what could I say, except that I was sorry? — though there was all that wonder in her face at having been brought in contact with so great a mystery. This new, undreamed-of, uncomfortable change was almost too much for her mind to recognize at all, but she had been shocked by it, and everything was different from what it used to be. She knew that at any rate.

"She said she was going to die," the child told me, still watching me with her sad and curious eyes as if everybody knew the secret of it all and would not tell her.

"You will know all about it when you are older, dear, and you will see her again by and by," I said; but she shook her head.

"She isn't coming back any more," she answered, as if she were sure of that at any rate.

There seemed to be no one to look after her, so presently I gave her some of my own luncheon. She was very hungry, and I pitied her more than ever, for the fact of her friendlessness grew more and more plain. She had pretty manners; she evidently had been brought up carefully, and there was a quaint dignity and reserve about her; she did nothing in a hurry, as if she had never been with other children at all and had learned no childish or impatient ways. I noticed her clothes, which were beginning to look worn and outgrown, but were very clean and well kept. It was on the edge of winter, but she still wore what must have been her last summer's hat, a little leghorn hat trimmed with white ribbon, and over her shoulders she had one of the very smallest of plaid shawls folded cornerwise, and pinned over neatly. She had some mittens, but she had taken those off and put them together on the window ledge.

Presently the conductor came in, evidently in a hurry, and when he saw that we had been lunching together he looked as if a weight were taken off his mind.

"I'm very much obliged to you," he said to me; "I meant to take her out and give her some dinner when we stopped, but I got a message that something had gone wrong up the road, and I had to fly round as fast 's I could. I only got part of a cup o' coffee myself."

"Is she under your care?" I asked.

The conductor moved the little girl to the seat facing mine, and bent over to tell me. "She's left all alone in the world. Father was a friend of mine, freight conductor on the road, and he was killed pretty near two years ago. Wife was a nice little woman, and the company helped her some, and she sewed and got along very well for a while, but she never had any health, and she died last Sunday of the pneumonia very sudden, — buried day before yesterday. The folks in the house sent a dispatch to a sister in Boston they'd heard her speak of, and she answered right off she'd take the child. They can't sell off what little stuff there is until they hear from her. My wife told me how things were and I spoke to the superintendent and said I'd take her on free, I believed. I'd a-taken her home myself and welcome, but long's she's got some folks of her own she'd better go to 'em. I don't much believe in fetching up other folks' children, but I told my wife last thing as I came out of the house that if I did n't like the looks of the woman that comes for her I'm just going to fetch her back again. She's the best little thing I ever saw; seems as if she knew what had happened and was trying to make the best of it. I found this Pullman was n't full, and I thought she could move round in here more than in one of the other cars. There ain't much travel at this time of year."

"I'll take the best care I can of her," said I; "I'm going to Boston"; and the conductor nodded and touched Nelly's cheek and disappeared.

She seemed to look upon everybody as her friend. She walked with unsteady, short steps to the other end of the car, and the bride, who was a pleasant-looking young woman, spoke to her kindly and gave her some candy; but I was sure that presently the child said, as she had said to me, that her mother was dead, for I saw the girl bend over her and flush a little, while her eyes filled with tears. I dare say she thought of her own mother whom she had so lately left, and she put her arm close round the child and kissed her, and afterwards seemed to be telling her a story at which Nelly smiled now and then.

I read for a while, but in the middle of the afternoon I fell asleep, and when I waked again the car lamps were lighted, and I looked for the little traveler, who was standing in the passageway of the car. She had taken off her hat, and there was evidently something wrong with it, for she was looking at it anxiously and trying to fasten something which had broken. I tried to beckon her to me, but in the seat just beside her was the priest, a stout, unsympathetic-looking old gentleman, and I was half amused and half touched to see her give the hat to him and show him where to fasten the strap of it. He was evidently much confused; he even blushed, but he did what she asked him with clumsy fingers and then put the hat on for her, as she stood before him and bent down her head as if he would have had to reach up to it. She was going away then, but he stopped her and gave her some bits of money from his pocket; she came a step or two nearer to him and held up her face to kiss him, and then he looked out of the window a minute and afterward turned and looked at his neighbors appealingly. It had been like a flower dropped into his prosaic life, I imagine; he was evidently quite surprised and pleased by so touching a confidence.

It must have been a long, dull day for a child to spend, but she was as good as possible, and did not give anybody the least trouble. We talked with each other about her, and felt as if she were under the care of every one of us. I could not help thinking how often we are at each other's mercy as we go through this world, and how much better it would be if we were as trustful and unsuspicious as this little child, and only looked for kindness at our neighbors' hands.

Just as it was growing dark she came to me and put her hand into mine and gave it a little pull.

"Come and see the birds," said she, and I suddenly became aware of the chirping of a robin somewhere near us. It was a funny sound to hear in the winter twilight, with the rattling of the train and shriek of the whistles, for it was really the note of a robin who was going to sleep on his nest in an apple-tree, or high

on an elm bough, some early summer evening. But
Nelly led me toward the old lady with so many bundles, and I found one of her treasures was a bird cage,
and there, sure enough, was the redbreast, a fat fellow
with smooth feathers, who winked and blinked at us
and stopped his chirping as we stood beside him.

"She seems pleased with him, the little girl does,"
said the bird's owner. "I'd like to have her see the
rest of my birds. Twenty-three I've got in all; thirteen of 'em's canaries. The woman in the other part
of the house is taking care of 'em while I'm gone.
I'm going on to Stockbridge to spend Thanksgiving
with my niece. It was a great piece o' work to get
started and I did n't feel at first 's if I could leave the
birds, but I knew Martha's folks would feel hurt if I
put 'em off again this year about coming. But I had
to take the old robin along with me. Some folks said
it might be the death of him, but he's never been one
mite scared. His cage stands in a window at home
where he sees a sight o' passing. He's the tamest thing
you ever saw. Now I'm so fur on my way I'm glad I
did make up my mind to start, though it'll be bad getting there in the night. I think a change is good for
anybody, and then I'm so tied down most of the time
with the birds that I don't get out much, and there's
nobody to fetch in the news."

"Why don't you bring up a few carrier pigeons with
the rest of your family?" said I, and this seemed to
amuse her very much.

"Sakes alive! I don't want no more," said she;
"but then I've said that all along; all the folks that
keeps canaries in our place comes to me if anything
ails 'em. Then I take 'em to doctor and get so attached to 'em I can't let 'em go again. I was telling

this little girl if I'd known I was going to see her I'd have brought along a nice little linnet for her; he'll sing all day long, but him and the one I put him with is always fighting each other, and all my other cages is too full a'ready. I reckon you'd be good to the little bird, would n't you now, dear?" The little traveler smiled eagerly, while I suddenly thought of the two sparrows that are sold for a farthing of this world's money.

I think we were all anxious to see what kind of woman the aunt would be, and I was half afraid she would look hard-hearted, and I knew in that case I should always be sorry when I thought of the little girl whose hand I was so sorry to let go. I had looked after her at night. I had waked a dozen times to look at her sweet little shadowed face as she slept, with the doll held fast in her arms.

At the station in the morning I found some one waiting to meet me, but I could not go until I saw the aunt. I waited with the conductor for a few minutes, and I was beginning to fear I must say good-by to my little traveler and never know her fortunes. Every one of the passengers had given her something, I believe — picture-papers and fruit and candy and I do not know what else — and I had seen even the old priest kiss her good-by most tenderly, and lay his hand on her head in what I am sure was a heartfelt blessing. I do not know whether it was some grand old Latin benediction, or a simple longing that God would be near to the lonely child and that His saints would defend her as she goes through the world.

I was glad when I saw just the woman I had wished and hoped for coming hurriedly toward us — there was no doubt that it was all right, she was sure of the child at a glance. I had fancied all the time that she must look like her mother.

"My dear baby!" the woman said with a sob, and caught her in her arms, while the little girl, with a quick, instinctive love, put out her short arms and they clung to each other without a word.

It was all right, as the conductor said again, half to himself and half to me. After a minute the woman said brokenly that she thanked him for his kindness. Poor Ellen! she never knew she was sick till the news came she was gone. He must tell the people out there that Nelly would have a good home. They stopped to talk longer and Nelly stood gravely by, but I had to hurry away, and after I was in the carriage I wished I could go back to kiss the little thing again.

QUESTIONS AND SUGGESTIONS

1. Tell just how the little girl looked and how she was dressed. How old do you think she was?
2. At what time in the year was the little traveler taking her long journey?
3. For whom do you think she was named?
4. Name five of the people who were on the train and tell something that each one did for the little traveler.
5. Why was every one so good to her?
6. What two sparrows are meant on page 32?
7. Why were the conductor and the writer so sure that the aunt was the right sort of woman?
8. I think that the writer of the story grew fonder of the little girl than any of the other travelers did. What do you think my reasons are?

THE CIRCUS AT DENBY

"The Circus at Denby" is taken from *Deephaven*, of which John G. Whittier once wrote to Miss Jewett, "I have read *Deephaven* over half a dozen times and always with gratitude to thee for such a book — so simple, pure, and so true to nature." Deephaven is a story of two girls from the city — dear friends — who spent a summer together in a dignified, old-fashioned house in a sea-port town in New England. One of the girls — Helen Denis — tells the story. The summer was full of happiness and quiet good times; and when the girls went away they left dear friends behind them. As you read the chapter see if you can find several reasons why they made so many friends.

KATE and I looked forward to a certain Saturday with as much eagerness as if we had been little schoolboys, for on that day we were to go to a circus at Denby, a town perhaps eight miles inland. There had not been a circus so near Deephaven for a long time, and nobody had dared to believe the first rumor of it, until two dashing young men had deigned to come themselves to put up the big posters on the end of 'Bijah Mauley's barn. All the boys in town came as soon as possible to see these amazing pictures, and some were wretched in their secret hearts at the thought that they might not see the show itself. Tommy Dockum was more interested than any one else, and mentioned the subject so frequently one day when he went blackberrying with us, that we grew enthusiastic, and told each other what fun it would be to go, for everybody would be there, and it would be the greatest loss to us if we were absent. I thought I had lost my childish fondness for circuses, but it came back redoubled. . . .

We felt that it was a great pity that any of the boys and girls should be left lamenting at home, and finding that there were some of our acquaintances and Tommy's who saw no chance of going, we engaged Jo Sands and Leander Dockum to carry them to Denby in two fish-wagons, with boards laid across for the extra seats. We saw them join the straggling train of carriages which had begun to go through the village from all along shore, soon after daylight, and they started on their journey shouting and carousing, with their pockets crammed with early apples and other provisions. We thought it would have been fun enough to see the people go by, for we had had no idea until then how many inhabitants that country held.

We had asked Mrs. Kew to go with us; but she was half an hour later than she had promised, for, since there was no wind, she could not come ashore in the sail-boat, and Mr. Kew had had to row her in in the dory. We saw the boat at last nearly in shore, and drove down to meet it: even the horse seemed to realize what a great day it was, and showed a disposition to friskiness, evidently as surprising to himself as to us.

Mrs. Kew was funnier that day than we had ever known her, which is saying a great deal, and we should not have had half so good a time if she had not been with us; although she lived in the lighthouse, and had no chance to "see passing," which a woman prizes so highly in the country, she had a wonderful memory for faces, and could tell us the names of all Deephaveners and of most of the people we met outside its limits. She looked impressed and solemn as she hurried up from the water's edge, giving Mr. Kew some parting charges over her shoulder as he pushed off the boat to go back; but after we had convinced her that the delay had not troubled us, she seemed more cheerful. It was evident that she felt the importance of the occasion, and that she was pleased at our having chosen her for company. She threw back her veil entirely, sat very straight, and took immense pains to bow to every acquaintance whom she met. She wore her best Sunday clothes, and her manner was formal for the first few minutes; it was evident that she felt we were meeting under unusual circumstances, and that, although we had often met before on the friendliest terms, our having asked her to make this excursion in public required a different sort of behavior at her hands, and a due amount of ceremony and propriety. But this state of things did not last long, as she soon made a remark at which Kate and I laughed so heartily in lighthouse-acquaintance fashion, that she unbent, and gave her whole mind to enjoying herself. . . .

We reached Denby at noon; it was an uninteresting town which had grown up around some mills. There was a great commotion in the streets, and it was evident that we had lost much in not having seen the procession. There was a great deal of business going on in the shops, and there were two or three hand-organs at large, near one of which we stopped awhile to listen, just after we had met Leander and given the horse into his charge. Mrs. Kew finished her shopping as soon as possible, and we hurried toward the great tents, where all the flags were flying. I think I have not told you that we were to have the benefit of seeing a menagerie in addition to the circus, and you may be sure we went faithfully round to see everything that the cages held.

I cannot truthfully say that it was a good show; it was somewhat dreary, now that I think of it quietly and without excitement. The creatures looked tired, and as if they had been on the road for a great many years. The animals were all old, and there was a shabby great elephant whose look of general discouragement went to my heart, for it seemed as if he were miserably conscious of a misspent life. He stood dejected and motionless at one side of the tent, and it was hard to believe that there was a spark of vitality left in him. A great number of the people had never seen an elephant before, and we heard a thin little old man, who stood near us, say delightedly, "There's the old creatur', and no mistake, Ann 'Liza. I wanted to see him most of anything. My sakes alive, ain't he big!"

And Ann 'Liza, who was stout and sleepy-looking, droned out, "Ye-es, there's consider'ble of him; but he looks as if he ain't got no animation."

Kate and I turned away and laughed, while Mrs. Kew said confidentially, as the couple moved away, "*She* need n't be a-reflectin' on the poor beast. That's Mis Seth Tanner, and there is n't a woman in Deephaven nor East Parish to be named the same day with her for laziness. I'm glad she did n't catch sight of me; she'd have talked about nothing for a fortnight."

There was a picture of a huge snake in Deephaven, and I was just wondering where he could be, or if there ever had been one, when we heard a boy ask the same question of the man whose thankless task it was to stir up the lions with a stick to make them roar. "The snake's dead," he answered good-naturedly. "Did n't you have to dig an awful long grave for him?" asked the boy; but the man said he reckoned they curled him up some, and smiled as he turned to his lions, who looked as if they needed a tonic. Everybody lingered longest before the monkeys, who seemed to be the only lively creatures in the whole collection; and finally we made our way into the other tent, and perched ourselves on a high seat, from whence we had a capital view of the audience and the ring, and could see the people come in. Mrs. Kew was on the lookout for acquaintances, and her spirits as well as our own seemed to rise higher and higher. She was on the alert, moving her head this way and that to catch sight of people, giving us a running commentary in the mean time. It was very pleasant to see a person so happy as Mrs. Kew was that day, and I dare say in speaking of the occasion she would say the same thing of Kate and me, — for it was such a good time! We bought some peanuts, without which no circus seems complete, and we listened to the conversations which were being carried on around us while we were waiting for the performance to begin. . . .

The circus was like all other circuses, except that it was shabbier than most, and the performers seemed to have less heart in it than usual. They did their best, and went through with their parts conscientiously, but they looked as if they never had had a good time in their lives. The audience was hilarious, and cheered and laughed at the tired clown until he looked as if he thought his speeches might possibly be funny, after all. We were so glad we had pleased the poor thing; and when he sang a song our satisfaction was still greater, and so he sang it all over again. Perhaps he had been associating with people who were used to circuses. . . .

"Does n't it seem as if you were a child again?"

Kate asked me. "I am sure this is just the same as the first circus I ever saw. It grows more and more familiar, and it puzzles me to think they should not have altered in the least while I have changed so much, and have even had time to grow up. . . .

"I remember," said Mrs. Kew, presently, "that just before I was married 'he' took me over to Wareham Corners to a caravan. My sister Hannah and the young man who was keeping company with her went too. I have n't been to one since till to-day, and it does carry me back same 's it does you, Miss Kate. It does n't seem more than five years ago, and what would I have thought if I had known 'he' and I were going to keep a lighthouse and be contented there, what 's more, and sometimes not get ashore for a fortnight; settled, gray-headed old folks! We were gay enough in those days. I know old Miss Sabrina Smith warned me that I 'd better think twice before I took up with Tom Kew, for he was a light-minded young man. I speak o' that to him in the winter-time, when he sets reading the almanac half asleep and I 'm knitting, and the wind 's a-howling and the waves coming ashore on those rocks as if they wished they could put out the light and blow down the lighthouse. We were reflected on a good deal for going to that caravan; some of the old folks did n't think it was improvin' — Well, I should think that man was a-trying to break his neck!"

Coming out of the great tent was disagreeable enough, and we seemed to have chosen the worst time, for the crowd pushed fiercely, though I suppose nobody was in the least hurry, and we were all severely jammed, while from somewhere underneath came the wails of a deserted dog. We had not meant to see the side-shows, and went carelessly past two or three tents; but when we came in sight of the picture of the Kentucky giantess, we noticed that Mrs. Kew looked at it wistfully, and we immediately asked if she cared anything about going to see the wonder, whereupon she confessed that she never heard of such a thing as a woman's weighing six hundred and fifty pounds, so we all three went in. There were only two or three persons inside the tent, beside a little boy who played the hand-organ.

The Kentucky giantess sat in two chairs on a platform, and there was a large cage of monkeys just beyond, toward which Kate and I went at once. "Why, she is n't more than two thirds as big as the picture," said Mrs. Kew, in a regretful whisper; "but I guess she 's big enough; does n't she look discouraged, poor creatur'?" Kate and I felt ashamed of ourselves for being there. No matter if she had consented to be carried round for a show, it must have been horrible to be stared at and joked about day after day; and we gravely looked at the monkeys, and in a few minutes turned to see if Mrs. Kew were not ready to come away, when to our surprise we saw that she was talking to the giantess with great interest, and we went nearer.

"I thought your face looked natural the minute I set foot inside the door," said Mrs. Kew; "but you 've — altered some since I saw you, and I could n't place you till I heard you speak. Why, you used to be spare; I am amazed, Marilly! Where are your folks?"

"I don't wonder you are surprised," said the giantess. "I was a good ways from this when you knew me, was n't I? But father he run through with every cent he had before he died, and 'he' took to drink

and it killed him after a while, and then I begun to
grow worse and worse, till I could n't do nothing to
earn a dollar, and everybody was a-coming to see me,
till at last I used to ask 'em ten cents apiece, and I
scratched along somehow till this man came round and
heard of me, and he offered me my keep and good pay
to go along with him. He had another giantess before
me, but she had begun to fall away consider'ble, so he
paid her off and let her go. This other giantess was
an awful expense to him, she was such an eater; now
I don't have no great of an appetite," — this was said
plaintively, — " and he's raised my pay since I've
been with him because we did so well. I took up with
his offer because I was nothing but a drag and never
will be. I'm as comfortable as I can be, but it's a
pretty hard business. My oldest boy is able to do for
himself, but he's married this last year, and his wife
don't want me. I don't know 's I blame her either. It
would be something like if I had a daughter now; but
there, I'm getting to like traveling first-rate; it gives
anybody a good deal to think of."

"I was asking the folks about you when I was up
home the early part of the summer," said Mrs. Kew,
"but all they knew was that you were living out in
New York State. Have you been living in Kentucky
long? I saw it on the picture outside."

"No," said the giantess, "that was a picture the
man bought cheap from another show that broke up
last year. It says six hundred and fifty pounds, but I
don't weigh more than four hundred. I have n't been
weighed for some time past. Between you and me I
don't weigh so much as that, but you must n't mention
it, for it would spoil my reputation, and might hender
my getting another engagement." And then the poor

giantess lost her professional look and tone as she said, "I believe I'd rather die than grow any bigger. I do lose heart sometimes, and wish I was a smart woman and could keep house. I'd be smarter than ever I was when I had the chance; I tell you that! Is Tom along with you?"

"No. I came with these young ladies, Miss Lancaster and Miss Denis, who are stopping over to Deephaven for the summer." Kate and I turned as we heard this introduction; we were standing close by, and I am proud to say that I never saw Kate treat any one more politely than she did that absurd, pitiful creature with the gilt crown and many bracelets. It was not that she said much, but there was such an exquisite courtesy in her manner, and an apparent unconsciousness of there being anything in the least surprising or uncommon about the giantess.

Just then a party of people came in, and Mrs. Kew said good-by reluctantly. "It has done me sights of good to see you," said our new acquaintance; "I was feeling down-hearted just before you came in. I'm pleased to see somebody that remembers me as I used to be." And they shook hands in a way that meant a great deal, and when Kate and I said good afternoon the giantess looked at us gratefully, and said, "I'm very much obliged to you for coming in, young ladies."

"Walk in! walk in!" the man was shouting as we came away. "Walk in and see the wonder of the world, ladies and gentlemen, — the largest woman ever seen in America, — the great Kentucky giantess!"

"Wouldn't you have liked to stay longer?" Kate asked Mrs. Kew as we came down the street. But she answered that it would be no satisfaction; the people were coming in, and she would have no chance to talk. "I never knew her very well; she is younger than I, and she used to go to meeting where I did, but she lived five or six miles from our house. She's had a hard time of it, according to her account," said Mrs. Kew. "She used to be a dreadful flighty, high-tempered girl, but she's lost that now, I can see by her eyes. I was running over in my mind to see if there was anything I could do for her, but I don't know as there is. She said the man who hired her was kind. I guess your treating her so polite did her as much good as anything. She used to be real ambitious. I had it on my tongue's end to ask her if she could n't get a few days' leave and come out to stop with me, but I thought just in time that she'd sink the dory in a minute. There! seeing her has took away all the fun," said Mrs. Kew ruefully; and we were all dismal for a while, but at last, after we were fairly started for home, we began to be merry again. . . .

We had a pleasant drive home, and we kept Mrs. Kew to supper, and afterward went down to the shore to see her set sail for home. Mr. Kew had come in some time before, and had been waiting for the moon to rise. Mrs. Kew told us that she should have enough to think of for a year, she had enjoyed the day so much; and we stood on the pebbles watching the boat out of the harbor, and wishing ourselves on board, it was such a beautiful evening. . . .

QUESTIONS AND SUGGESTIONS

1. Tell all you can about Mrs. Kew and life at the lighthouse. You would be greatly interested in another chapter in the story, called "The Lighthouse."

2. How would girls who were less kind-hearted and well-

bred than Kate and Helen have acted when they went into the tent of the Kentucky giantess?

3. Why was Helen proud of Kate?

4. It often happens that funny and sorrowful things are very closely bound up together. Sometimes the same thing is both funny and touching. Find a good illustration of this in this story.

THE NIGHT BEFORE THANKSGIVING

"The Night before Thanksgiving" occurs in Miss Jewett's last volume of short stories, *The Queen's Twin and Other Stories*. You would enjoy many of the stories in this volume, especially "The Queen's Twin" and "The Coon Dog." There is a very sweet and humorous little Irish story in the collection, called "Bold Words at the Bridge"; and in the story called "Aunt Cynthy Dallett" is an incidental account of a New England woman's perverted notion of hospitality, which is deliciously humorous and worth reading and discussing even without the rest of the story.

It is very interesting to find how much Miss Jewett has made us see in this little Thanksgiving story without writing long descriptions. After reading the story, you may be interested to answer questions 1, 2, 3, and 4 to prove this.

A good short-story writer does not talk a great deal about the people in the story, but makes us acquainted with them by telling us what they do and say. After reading, answer questions 5, 6, 7, and 8 with this in mind.

I

THERE was a sad heart in the low-storied, dark little house that stood humbly by the roadside under some tall elms. Small as her house was, old Mrs. Robb found it too large for herself alone; she only needed the kitchen and a tiny bedroom that led out of it, and there still remained the best room and a bedroom, with the low garret overhead.

There had been a time, after she was left alone, when Mrs. Robb could help those who were poorer than herself. She was strong enough not only to do a woman's work inside her house, but almost a man's work outside in her piece of garden ground. At last sickness and age had come hand in hand, those two relentless enemies of the poor, and together they had wasted her strength and substance. She had always been looked up to by her neighbors as being independent, but now she was left, lame-footed and lame-handed, with a debt to carry and her bare land, and the house ill provisioned to stand the siege of time.

For a while she managed to get on, but at last it began to be whispered about that there was no use for any one so proud; it was easier for the whole town to care for her than for a few neighbors, and Mrs. Robb had better go to the poorhouse before winter, and be done with it. At this terrible suggestion her brave heart seemed to stand still. The people whom she cared for most happened to be poor, and she could no longer go into their households to make herself of use. The very elms overhead seemed to say, "Oh, no!" as they groaned in the late autumn winds, and there was something appealing even to the strange passer-by in the look of the little gray house, with Mrs. Robb's pale worried face at the window.

II

Some one has said that anniversaries are days to make other people happy in, but sometimes when they come they seem to be full of shadows, and the power of giving joy to others, that inalienable right which ought to lighten the saddest heart, the most indifferent sympathy, sometimes even this seems to be withdrawn.

So poor old Mary Ann Robb sat at her window on the afternoon before Thanksgiving and felt herself poor and sorrowful indeed. Across the frozen road she looked eastward over a great stretch of cold meadow land, brown and wind-swept and crossed by icy ditches. It seemed to her as if before this, in all the troubles that she had known and carried, there had always been some hope to hold: as if she had never looked poverty full in the face and seen its cold and pitiless look before. She looked anxiously down the road, with a horrible shrinking and dread at the thought of being asked, out of pity, to join in some Thanksgiving feast, but there was nobody coming with gifts in hand. Once she had been full of love for such days, whether at home or abroad, but something chilled her very heart now.

Her nearest neighbor had been foremost of those who wished her to go to the town farm, and he had said more than once that it was the only sensible thing. But John Mander was waiting impatiently to get her tiny farm into his own hands; he had advanced some money upon it in her extremity, and pretended that there was still a debt, after he cleared her wood lot to pay himself back. He would plough over the graves in the field corner and fell the great elms, and waited now like a spider for his poor prey. He often reproached her for being too generous to worthless people in the past and coming to be a charge to others now. Oh, if she could only die in her own house and not suffer the pain of homelessness and dependence!

It was just at sunset, and as she looked out hopelessly across the gray fields, there was a sudden gleam of light far away on the low hills beyond; the clouds opened in the west and let the sunshine through. One lovely gleam shot swift as an arrow and brightened a far cold hillside where it fell, and at the same moment a sudden gleam of hope brightened the winter landscape of her heart.

"There was Johnny Harris," said Mary Ann Robb softly. "He was a soldier's son, left an orphan and distressed. Old John Mander scolded, but I could n't see the poor boy in want. I kept him that year after he got hurt, spite o' what anybody said, an' he helped me what little he could. He said I was the only mother he'd ever had. 'I'm goin' out West, Mother Robb,' says he. 'I sha' n't come back till I get rich,' an' then he'd look at me an' laugh, so pleasant and boyish. He wa'n't one that liked to write. I don't think he was doin' very well when I heard,— there, it's most four years ago now. I always thought if he got sick or anything, I should have a good home for him to come to. There's poor Ezra Blake, the deaf one, too,— he won't have any place to welcome him."

The light faded out of doors, and again Mrs. Robb's troubles stood before her. Yet it was not so dark as it had been in her sad heart. She still sat by the window, hoping now, in spite of herself, instead of fearing; and a curious feeling of nearness and expectancy made her feel not so much light-hearted as light-headed.

"I feel just as if somethin' was goin' to happen," she said. "Poor Johnny Harris, perhaps he's thinkin' o' me, if he's alive."

It was dark now out of doors, and there were tiny clicks against the window. It was beginning to snow, and the great elms creaked in the rising wind overhead.

III

A dead limb of one of the old trees had fallen that autumn, and, poor firewood as it might be, it was Mrs. Robb's own, and she had burnt it most thankfully. There was only a small armful left, but at least she could have the luxury of a fire. She had a feeling that it was her last night at home, and with strange recklessness began to fill the stove as she used to do in better days.

"It 'll get me good an' warm," she said, still talking to herself, as lonely people do, "an' I 'll go to bed early. It 's comin' on to storm."

The snow clicked faster and faster against the window, and she sat alone thinking in the dark.

"There 's lots of folks I love," she said once. "They 'd be sorry I ain't got nobody to come, an' no supper the night afore Thanksgivin'. I 'm dreadful glad they don't know." And she drew a little nearer to the fire, and laid her head back drowsily in the old rocking-chair.

It seemed only a moment before there was a loud knocking, and somebody lifted the latch of the door. The fire shone bright through the front of the stove and made a little light in the room, but Mary Ann Robb waked up frightened and bewildered.

"Who 's there?" she called, as she found her crutch and went to the door. She was only conscious of her one great fear. "They 've come to take me to the poorhouse!" she said, and burst into tears.

There was a tall man, not John Mander, who seemed to fill the narrow doorway.

"Come, let me in!" he said gayly. "It 's a cold night. You did n't expect me, did you, Mother Robb?"

"Dear me, what is it?" she faltered, stepping back as he came in, and dropping her crutch. "Be I dreamin'? I was a-dreamin' about— Oh, there! What was I a-sayin'? 'T ain't true! No! I 've made some kind of a mistake."

Yes, and this was the man who kept the poorhouse,

and she would go without complaint; they might have given her notice, but she must not fret.

"Sit down, sir," she said, turning toward him with touching patience. "You'll have to give me a little time. If I'd been notified I would n't have kept you waiting a minute this stormy night."

It was not the keeper of the poorhouse. The man by the door took one step forward and put his arm round her and kissed her.

"What are you talking about?" said John Harris. "You ain't goin' to make me feel like a stranger? I've come all the way from Dakota to spend Thanksgivin'. There's all sorts o' things out here in the wagon, an' a man to help get 'em in. Why, don't cry so, Mother Robb. I thought you'd have a great laugh, if I come and surprised you. Don't you remember I always said I should come?"

It was John Harris, indeed. The poor soul could say nothing. She felt now as if her heart was going to break with joy. He left her in the rocking-chair and came and went in his old boyish way, bringing in the store of gifts and provisions. It was better than any dream. He laughed and talked, and went out to send away the man to bring a wagonful of wood from John Mander's, and came in himself laden with pieces of the nearest fence to keep the fire going in the mean time. They must cook the beefsteak for supper right away; they must find the pound of tea among all the other bundles; they must get good fires started in both the cold bedrooms. Why, Mother Robb did n't seem to be ready for company from out West! The great, cheerful fellow hurried about the tiny house, and the little old woman limped after him, forgetting everything but hospitality. Had not she a house for John to come to?

THE NIGHT BEFORE THANKSGIVING

Were not her old chairs and tables in their places still? And he remembered everything, and kissed her as they stood before the fire, as if she were a girl.

He had found plenty of hard times, but luck had come at last. He had struck luck, and this was the end of a great year.

"No, I couldn't seem to write letters; no use to complain o' the worst, an' I wanted to tell you the best when I came"; and he told it while she cooked the supper. "No, I wa'n't goin' to write no foolish letters," John repeated. He was afraid he should cry himself when he found out how bad things had been; and they sat down to supper together, just as they used to do when he was a homeless orphan boy, whom nobody else wanted in winter weather while he was crippled and could not work. She could not be kinder now than she was then, but she looked so poor and old! He saw her taste her cup of tea and set it down again with a trembling hand and a look at him. " No, I wanted to come myself," he blustered, wiping his eyes and trying to laugh. "And you're going to have everything you need to make you comfortable long's you live, Mother Robb!"

She looked at him again and nodded, but she did not even try to speak. There was a good hot supper ready, and a happy guest had come; it was the night before Thanksgiving.

QUESTIONS AND SUGGESTIONS

1. Describe Mrs. Robb's house as it would have looked to a passer-by.
2. What could she see from the front window?
3. Draw a ground-plan of the house.

4. If you had walked through the field beside the house, what should you have found there?

5. Read what Mrs. Robb said to herself as she drew her chair up in front of the fire. If this were all we were told about her, what should we know of her character?

6. Read what she says to the man whom she takes to be the poorhouse keeper. What does this show us?

7. Find one of the ways in which Miss Jewett tells us how glad Mother Robb was to have John Harris back again.

8. How do you know that John Harris was loyal, generous, tender-hearted? How could he have let so long a time go by without writing to Mother Robb?

9. How does the first sentence in the story make you feel? The last sentence?

10. What is the first sentence in the story that makes you begin to be hopeful?

11. What verse from the Bible would make a good name for the story?

A WAR DEBT

"A War Debt" is in one of Miss Jewett's latest and best volumes, *The Life of Nancy*. You would enjoy almost every story in this book: some are sad, some are amusing, all help us to understand life better and to feel more kindly towards "all sorts and conditions of men." You would love "The Life of Nancy" and would have a good laugh over "The Guests of Mrs. Tims" and "Fame's Little Day." The story called "The Hiltons' Holiday" is one of the most exquisite Miss Jewett ever wrote and is a great favorite among grown-up people, although it is written about children.

"A War Debt" is chosen for you because it deals with a period of American history in which you are especially interested, — the Civil War. Another good story by Miss Jewett dealing with the same event, but from a very different point of view, is "Decoration Day," in the volume entitled "A Native of Winby." In "Strangers and Wayfarers" there is a very touching story picturing the South after the war, called "The Mistress of Sydenham Plantation." It would be quite worth while for you to read both of these.

I

THERE was a tinge of autumn color on even the English elms as Tom Burton walked slowly up Beacon Street. He was wondering all the way what he had better do with himself; it was far too early to settle down in Boston for the winter, but his grandmother kept to her old date for moving up to town, and here they were. As yet nobody thought of braving the country weather long after October came in, and most country houses were poorly equipped with fire-places, or even furnaces: this was some years ago, and not the very last autumn that ever was.

There was likely to be a long stretch of good weather, a month at least, if one took the trouble to go a little way to the southward. Tom Burton quickened his steps a little, and began to think definitely of his guns, while a sudden resolve took shape in his mind. Just then he reached the doorsteps of his grandmother's fine old-fashioned house, being himself the fourth Thomas Burton that the shining brass door-plate had represented. His old grandmother was the only near relative he had in the world; she was growing older and more dependent upon him every day. That summer he had returned from a long wandering absence of three years, and the vigorous elderly woman whom he had left, busy and self-reliant, had sadly changed in the mean time; age had begun to strike telling blows at her strength and spirits. Tom had no idea of leaving her again for the long journeys which had become the delightful habit of his life; but there was no reason why he should not take a fortnight's holiday now and then, particularly now.

"Has Mrs. Burton come down yet, Dennis? Is there any one with her?" asked Tom, as he entered.

"There is not, sir. Mrs. Burton is in the drawing-room," answered Dennis precisely. "The tea is just going up; I think she was waiting for you." And Tom ran upstairs like a schoolboy, and then walked discreetly into the drawing-room. His grandmother gave no sign of having expected him, but she always liked company at that hour of the day: there had come to be too many ghosts in the empty chairs.

"Can I have two cups?" demanded the grandson,

cheerfully. "I don't know when I have had such a walk!" and they began a gay gossiping hour together, and parted for a short season afterward, only to meet again at dinner, with a warm sense of pleasure in each other's company. The young man always insisted that his grandmother was the most charming woman in the world, and it can be imagined what the grandmother thought of Tom. She was only severe with him because he had given no signs of wishing to marry, but she was tolerant of all delay, so long as she could now and then keep the subject fresh in his mind. It was not a moment to speak again of the great question that afternoon, and she had sat and listened to his talk of people and things, a little plaintive and pale, but very handsome, behind the tea-table.

II

At dinner, after Dennis had given Tom his cup of coffee and cigars, and disappeared with an accustomed air of thoughtfully leaving the family alone for a private interview, Mrs. Burton, who sometimes lingered if she felt like talking, and sometimes went away to the drawing-room to take a brief nap before she began her evening book, and before Tom joined her for a few minutes to say good-night if he were going out,— Mrs. Burton left her chair more hurriedly than usual. Tom meant to be at home that evening, and was all ready to speak of his plan for some Southern shooting, and he felt a sudden sense of disappointment.

"Don't go away," he said, looking up as she passed. "Is this a bad cigar?"

"No, no, my dear," said the old lady, hurrying across the room in an excited, unusual sort of way. "I wish to show you something while we are by ourselves." And she stooped to unlock a little cupboard in the great sideboard, and fumbled in the depths there, upsetting and clanking among some pieces of silver. Tom joined her with a pair of candles, but it was some moments before she could find what she wanted. Mrs. Burton appeared to be in a hurry, which almost never happened, and in trying to help her Tom dropped much wax unheeded at her side.

"Here it is at last," she said, and went back to her seat at the table. "I ought to tell you the stories of some old silver that I keep in that cupboard; if I were to die, nobody would know anything about them."

"Do you mean the old French spoons, and the prince's porringer, and those things?" asked Tom, showing the most lively interest. But his grandmother was busy unfastening the strings of a little bag, and shook her head absently in answer to his question. She took out and handed to him a quaint old silver cup with two handles, that he could not remember ever to have seen.

"What a charming old bit!" said he, turning it about. "Where in the world did it come from? English, of course; and it looks like a loving-cup. A copy of some old Oxford thing, perhaps; only they did n't copy much then. I should think it had been made for a child." Tom turned it round and round and drew the candles toward him. "Here's an inscription, too, but very much worn."

"Put it down a minute," said Mrs. Burton impatiently. "Every time I have thought of it I have been more and more ashamed to have it in the house. People were n't so shocked by such things at first; they would only be sentimental about the ruined homes, and say that 'after all, it was the fortune of war.' That cup was stolen."

"But who stole it?" inquired Tom, with deep interest.

"Your father brought it here," said Mrs. Burton, with great spirit, and even a tone of reproach. "My son, Tom Burton, your father, brought it home from the war. I think his plan was to keep it safe to send back to the owners. But he left it with your mother when he was ordered suddenly to the front; he was only at home four days, and the day after he got back to camp was the day he was killed, poor boy"—

"I remember something about it now," Tom hastened to say. "I remember my mother's talking about the breaking up of Southern homes, and all that; she never believed it until she saw the cup, and I thought it was awfully silly. I was at the age when I could have blown our own house to pieces just for the sake of the racket."

"And that terrible year your grandfather's and your mother's death followed, and I was left alone with you — two of us out of the five that had made my home"—

"I should say one and a half," insisted Tom, with some effort. "What a boy I was for a grandson! Thank Heaven, there comes a time when we are all the same age! We are jolly together now, are n't we? Come, dear old lady, don't let's think too much of what's gone by"; and he went round the table and gave her a kiss, and stood there where she need not look him in the face, holding her dear thin hand as long as ever she liked.

"I want you to take that silver cup back, Tom," she said presently, in her usual tone. "Go back and finish your coffee." She had seldom broken down like this. Mrs. Burton had been self-possessed, even to apparent coldness, in earlier life.

"How in the world am I going to take it back?" asked Tom, most businesslike and calm. "Do you really know just where it came from? And then it was several years ago."

"Your grandfather knew; they were Virginia people, of course, and happened to be old friends; one of the younger men was his own classmate. He knew the crest and motto at once, but there were two or three branches of the family, none of them, so far as he knew, living anywhere near where your father was in camp. Poor Tom said that there was a beautiful old house sacked and burnt, and everything scattered that was saved. He happened to hear a soldier from another regiment talking about it, and saw him tossing this cup about, and bought it from him with all the money he happened to have in his pockets."

"Then he did n't really steal it himself!" exclaimed Tom, laughing a little, and with a sense of relief.

"No no, Tom!" said Mrs. Burton impatiently. "Only you see that it really is a stolen thing, and I have had it all this time under my roof. For a long time it was packed away with your father's war relics, those things that I could n't bear to see. And then I would think of it only at night after I had once seen it, and forget to ask any one else while you were away, or wait for you to come. Oh, I have no excuse. I have been very careless, but here it has been all the time. I wish you would find out about the people; there must be some one belonging to them — some friend, perhaps, to whom we could give it. This is one of the things that I wish to have done, and to forget. Just take it back, or write some letters first: you will know what to do. I should like to have the people understand."

"I'll see about it at once," said Tom, with great zest. "I believe you could n't have spoken at a better time. I have been thinking of going down to Virginia this very week. I hear that they are in a hurry with fitting out that new scientific expedition in Washington that I declined to join, and they want me to come on and talk over things before they are off. One of the men is a Virginian, an awfully good fellow; and then there's Clendennin, my old chum, who's in Washington, too, just now; they'll give me my directions; they know all Virginia between them. I'll take the cup along, and run down from Washington for a few days, and perhaps get some shooting."

Tom's face was shining with interest and satisfaction; he took the cup and again held it under the candle-light. "How pretty this old chasing is round the edge, and the set of the little handles! Oh, here's the motto! What a dear old thing, and enormously old! See here, under the crest," and he held it toward Mrs. Burton: —

Je vous en prie
Bel-ami.

Mrs. Burton glanced at it with indifference. "Yes, it is charming, as you say. But I only wish to return it to its owners, Tom."

"*Je vous en prie*
Bel-ami."

Tom repeated the words under his breath, and looked at the crest carefully.

"I remember that your grandfather said it belonged

to the Bellamys," said his grandmother. "Of course: how could I forget that! I have never looked at it properly since the day I first saw it. It is a charming motto — they were very charming and distinguished people. I suppose this is a pretty way of saying that they could not live without their friends. I beg of you, Belami; it is a quaint fancy; one might turn it in two or three pretty ways."

"Or they may have meant that they only looked to themselves for what they wanted, *Je vous en prie Bellamy!*" said Tom gallantly. "All right; I think that I shall start to-morrow or next day. If you have no special plans," he added.

"Do go, my dear; you may get some shooting, as you say," said Mrs. Burton, a little wistfully, but kindly personifying Tom's inclination.

"You've started me off on a fine romantic adventure," said the young man, smiling. "Come; my cigar's gone out, and it never was good for much; let's go in and try the cards, and talk about things; perhaps you'll think of something more about the Bellamys. You said that my grandfather had a classmate " —

Mrs. Burton stopped to put the cup into its chamois bag again, and handed it solemnly to Tom; then she took his arm, and dismissing all unpleasant thoughts, they sat down to the peaceful game of cribbage to while away the time. The grandson lent himself gayly to pleasure-making, and they were just changing the cards for their books, when one of the elder friends of the house appeared, one of the two or three left who called Mrs. Burton Margaret, and was greeted affectionately as Henry in return. This guest always made the dear lady feel young; he himself was always to the front of things, and had much to say. It was quite forgotten that a last charge had been given to Tom, or that the past had been wept over. Presently, the late evening hours being always her best, she forgot in eager talk that she had any grandson at all, and Tom slipped away with his book to his own sitting-room and his pipe. He took the little cup out of its bag again, and set it before him, and began to lay plans for a Southern journey.

III

The Virginia country was full of golden autumn sunshine and blue haze. The long hours spent on a slow-moving train were full of shocks and surprises to a young traveler who knew almost every civilized country better than his own. The lonely look of the fields, the trees shattered by war, which had not yet had time enough to muffle their broken tops with green; the negroes, who crowded on board the train, lawless, and unequal to holding their liberty with steady hands, looked poor and less respectable than in the old plantation days — it was as if the long discipline of their former state had counted for nothing. Tom Burton felt himself for the first time to have something of a statesman's thoughts and schemes as he moralized along the way. Presently he noticed with deep sympathy a lady who came down the crowded car, and took the seat just in front of him. She carried a magazine under her arm — a copy of "Blackwood," which was presently proved to bear the date of 1851, and to be open at an article on the death of Wordsworth. She was the first lady he had seen that day — there was little money left for journeying and pleasure among the white Virginians; but two or three stations beyond this a group of young English men and women stood with the gay negroes on the platform, and came into the train with cheerful greetings to their friends. It seemed as if England had begun to settle Virginia all over again, and their clear, lively voices had no foreign sound. There were going to be races at some courthouse town in the neighborhood. Burton was a great lover of horses himself, and the new scenes grew more and more interesting. In one of the gay groups was a different figure from any of the fresh-cheeked young wives of the English planters — a slender girl, pale and spirited, with a look of care beyond her years. She was the queen of her little company. It was to her that every one looked for approval and sympathy as the laugh went to and fro. There was something so high-bred and elegant in her bearing, something so exquisitely sure and stately, that her companions were made clumsy and rustic in their looks by contrast. The eager talk of the coming races, of the untried thoroughbreds, the winners and losers of the year before, made more distinct this young Virginia lady's own look of high breeding, and emphasized her advantage of race. She was the newer and finer Norman among Saxons. She alone seemed to have that inheritance of swiftness of mind, of sureness of training. It was the highest type of English civilization refined still further by long growth in favoring soil. Tom Burton read her unconscious face as if it were a romance; he believed that one of the great Virginia houses must still exist, and that she was its young mistress. The house's fortune was no doubt gone; the long-worn and carefully mended black silk gown that followed the lines of her lovely figure told plainly enough that worldly prosperity was a thing of the past. But what nature could give of its best, and only age and death could take away, were hers. He watched her more and more; at one moment she glanced up suddenly and held his eyes with hers for one revealing moment. There was no surprise in the look, but a confession of pathos, a recognition of sympathy, which made even a stranger feel that he had the inmost secret of her heart.

IV

The next day our hero, having hired a capital saddle-horse, a little the worse for age, was finding his way eastward along the sandy roads. The country was full of color; the sassafras and gum trees and oaks were all ablaze with red and yellow. Now and then he caught a glimpse of a sail on one of the wide reaches of the river which lay to the northward; now and then he passed a broken gateway or the ruins of a cabin. He carried a light gun before him across the saddle, and a game-bag hung slack and empty at his shoulder except for a single plump partridge in one corner, which had whirred up at the right moment out of a vine-covered thicket. Something small and heavy in his coat pocket seemed to correspond to the bird, and once or twice he unconsciously lifted it in the hollow of his hand. The day itself, and a sense of being on the road to fulfill his mission, a sense of unending leisure and satisfaction under that lovely hazy sky, seemed to leave no place for impatience or thought of other things. He rode slowly along, with his eye on the roadside coverts, letting the horse take his own gait, except when a ragged negro boy, on an unwilling, heavy-footed mule, slyly approached and struck the dallying steed from behind. It was past the middle of the October afternoon.

"'Mos' thar now, Cun'l," said the boy at last, eagerly. "See them busted trees pas' thar, an' chimblies?

You tu'n down nax' turn; ride smart piece yet, an' you come right front of ol' Mars Bell'my's house. See, he comin' 'long de road now. Yas, 't is Mars Bell'my shore, an' 's gun."

Tom had been looking across the neglected fields with compassion, and wondering if such a plantation could ever be brought back to its days of prosperity. As the boy spoke he saw the tall chimneys in the distance, and then, a little way before him in the shadow of some trees, a stately figure that slowly approached. He hurriedly dismounted, leading his horse until he met the tall old man, who answered his salutation with much dignity. There was something royal and remote from ordinary men in his silence after the first words of courteous speech.

"Yas, sir; that's Mars Bell'my, sir," whispered the boy on the mule, reassuringly, and the moment of hesitation was happily ended.

"I was on my way to call upon you, Colonel Bellamy; my name is Burton," said the younger man.

"Will you come with me to the house?" said the old gentleman, putting out his hand cordially a second time; and though he had frowned slightly at first at the unmistakable Northern accent, the light came quickly to his eyes. Tom gave his horse's bridle to the boy, who promptly transferred himself to the better saddle, and began to lead the mule instead.

"I have been charged with an errand of friendship," said Tom. "I believe that you and my grandfather were at Harvard together." Tom looked boyish and eager and responsive to hospitality at this moment. He was straight and trim, like a Frenchman. Colonel Bellamy was much the taller of the two, even with his bent shoulders and relaxed figure.

"I see the resemblance to your grandfather, sir. I bid you welcome to Fairford," said the Colonel. "Your visit is a great kindness."

They walked on together, speaking ceremoniously of the season and of the shooting and Tom's journey, until they left the woods and overgrown avenue at the edge of what had once been a fine lawn, with clusters of huge oaks; but these were shattered by war and more or less ruined. The lopped trunks still showed the marks of fire and shot; some had put out a fresh bough or two, but most of the ancient trees stood for their own monuments, rain-bleached and gaunt. At the other side of the wide lawn, against young woodland and a glimpse of the river, were the four great chimneys which had been seen from the highroad. There was no dwelling in sight at the moment, and Tom stole an apprehensive look at the grave face of his companion. It appeared as if he were being led to the habitation of ghosts, as if he were purposely to be confronted with the desolation left in the track of Northern troops. It was not so long since the great war that these things could be forgotten.

The Colonel, however, without noticing the ruins in any way, turned toward the right as he neared them; and passing a high fragment of brick wall topped by a marble ball or two — which had been shot at for marks — and passing, just beyond, some huge clumps of box, they came to a square brick building with a rude wooden addition at one side, and saw some tumble-down sheds a short distance beyond this, with a negro cabin.

They came to the open door. "This was formerly the billiard-room. Your grandfather would have kept many memories of it," said the host simply. "Will you go in, Mr. Burton?" And Tom climbed two or three perilous wooden steps and entered, to find himself in a most homelike and charming place. There was a huge fireplace opposite the door, with a thin whiff of blue smoke going up, a few old books on the high chimney-piece, a pair of fine portraits with damaged frames, some old tables and chairs of different patterns, with a couch by the square window covered with a piece of fine tapestry folded together and still showing its beauty, however raveled and worn. By the opposite window, curtained only by vines, sat a lady with her head muffled in lace, who greeted the guest pleasantly, and begged pardon for not rising from her chair. Her face wore an unmistakable look of pain and sorrow. As Tom Burton stood at her side, he could find nothing to say in answer to her apologies. He was not wont to be abashed, and a real court could not affect him like this ideal one. The poor surroundings could only be seen through the glamour of their owner's presence — it seemed a most elegant interior.

"I am sorry to have the inconvenience of deafness," said Madam Bellamy, looking up with an anxious little smile. "Will you tell me again the name of our guest?"

"He is my old classmate Burton's grandson, of Boston," said the Colonel, who now stood close at her side; he looked apprehensive as he spoke, and the same shadow flitted over his face as when Tom had announced himself by the oak at the roadside.

"I remember Mr. Burton, your grandfather, very well," said Madam Bellamy at last, giving Tom her hand for the second time, as her husband had done. "He was your guest here the autumn before we were married, my dear; a fine rider, I remember, and a charming gentleman. He was much entertained by one of our hunts. I saw that you also carried a gun. My dear," and she turned to her husband anxiously, "did you bring home any birds?"

Colonel Bellamy's face lengthened. "I had scarcely time, or perhaps I had not my usual good fortune," said he. "The birds have followed the grain-fields away from Virginia, we sometimes think."

"I can offer you a partridge," said Tom eagerly. "I shot one as I rode along. I am afraid that I stopped Colonel Bellamy just as he was going out."

"I thank you very much," said Madam Bellamy. "And you will take supper with us, certainly. You will give us the pleasure of a visit? I regret very much my granddaughter's absence, but it permits me to offer you her room, which happens to be vacant." But Tom attempted to make excuse. "No, no," said Madam Bellamy, answering her own thoughts rather than his words. "You must certainly stay the night with us; we shall make you most welcome. It will give my husband great pleasure; he will have many questions to ask you."

Tom went out to search for his attendant, who presently clattered away on the mule at an excellent homeward pace. An old negro manservant led away the horse, and Colonel Bellamy disappeared also, leaving the young guest to entertain himself and his hostess for an hour, that flew by like light. A woman who is charming in youth is still more charming in age to a man of Tom Burton's imagination, and he was touched to find how quickly the first sense of receiving an antagonist had given way before a desire to show their feeling of kindly hospitality toward a guest. The links of ancient friendship still held strong, and as Tom sat with his hostess by the window they had much pleasant talk of Northern families known to them both, of whom, or of whose children and grandchildren, he could give much news. It seemed as if he should have known Madam Bellamy all his life. It is impossible to say how she illumined her poor habitation, with what dignity and sweetness she avoided, as far as possible, any reference to the war or its effects. One could hardly remember that she was poor, or ill, or had suffered such piteous loss of friends and fortune.

Later, when Tom was walking toward the river through the woods and overgrown fields of the plantation, he came upon the ruins of the old cabins of what must have been a great family of slaves. The crumbling heaps of the chimneys stood in long lines on either side of a weed-grown lane; not far beyond he found the sinking mounds of some breastworks on a knoll which commanded the river channel. The very trees and grass looked harrowed and distressed by war; the silence of the sunset was only broken by the cry of a little owl that was begging mercy of its fears far down the lonely shore.

V

At supper that night Burton came from his room to find Colonel Bellamy bringing his wife in his arms to the table, while the old bent-backed and gray-headed manservant followed to place her chair. The mistress of Fairford was entirely lame and helpless, but she sat at the head of her table like a queen. There was a bunch of damask roses at her plate. The Colonel himself was in evening dress, antique in cut, and sadly worn, and Tom heartily thanked his patron saint that the boy had brought his portmanteau in good season.

There was a glorious light in the room from the fire, and the table was served with exquisite care, and even more luxurious delay, the excellent fish which the Colonel himself must have caught in his unexplained absence, and Tom's own partridge, which was carved as if it had been the first wild turkey of the season, were followed by a few peaches touched with splendid color as they lay on a handful of leaves in a bent and dented pewter plate. There seemed to be no use for the stray glasses, until old Milton produced a single small bottle of beer, and uncorked and poured it for his master and his master's guest with a grand air. The Colonel lifted his eyebrows slightly, but accepted its appearance at the proper moment.

They sat long at table. It was impossible to let one's thought dwell upon any of the meagre furnishings of the feast. The host and hostess talked of the days when they went often to France and England, and of Tom's grandfather when he was young. At last Madam Bellamy left the table, and Tom stood waiting while she was carried to her own room. He had kissed her hand like a courtier as he said goodnight. On the Colonel's return the old butler ostentatiously placed the solitary bottle between them and went away. The Colonel offered some excellent tobacco, and Tom begged leave to fetch his pipe. When he returned he brought with it the chamois-skin bag that held the silver cup, and laid it before him on the table. It was like the dread of going into battle, but the moment had arrived. He laid his hand on the cup for a moment as if to hide it, then he waited until his pipe was fairly going.

"This is something which I have come to restore to you, sir," said Tom presently, taking the piece of silver from its wrappings. "I believe that it is your property."

The old Colonel's face wore a strange, alarmed look; his thin cheeks grew crimson. He reached eagerly for the cup, and held it before his eyes. At last he bent his head and kissed it. Tom Burton saw that his tears began to fall, that he half rose, turning toward the door of the next room, where his wife was; then he sank back again, and looked at his guest appealingly.

"I ask no questions," he faltered; "it was the fortune of war. This cup was my grandfather's, my father's, and mine; all my own children drank from it in turn; they are all gone before me. We always called it our lucky cup. I fear that it has come back too late" — The old man's voice broke, but he still held the shining piece of silver before him, and turned it about in the candle-light.

"*Je vous en prie Bel-ami,*"

he whispered under his breath, and put the cup before him on the scarred mahogany.

VI

"Shall we move our chairs before the fire, Mr. Burton? My dear wife is but frail," said the old man, after a long silence, and with touching pathos. "She sees me companioned for the evening, and is glad to seek her room early; if you were not here she would insist upon our game of cards. I do not allow myself to dwell upon the past, and I have no wish for gay company." He added, in a lower voice, "My daily dread in life is to be separated from her."

As the evening wore on, the autumn air grew chilly, and again and again the host replenished his draughty fireplace, and pushed the box of delicious tobacco toward his guest, and Burton in his turn ventured to remember a flask in his portmanteau, and begged the Colonel to taste it, because it had been filled from an old cask in his grandfather's cellar. The butler's eyes shone with satisfaction when he was unexpectedly called upon to brew a little punch after the old Fairford fashion, and the later talk ranged along the youthful escapades of Thomas Burton the elder to the beauties and the style of Addison; from the latest improvement in shot-guns to the statesmanship of Thomas Jefferson, while the Colonel spoke tolerantly, in passing, of some slight misapprehensions of Virginia life made by a delightful young writer, too early lost — Mr. Thackeray.

Tom Burton had never enjoyed an evening more; the romance, the pathos of it, as he found himself more and more taking his grandfather's place in the mind of this hereditary friend, waked all his sympathy. The charming talk that never dwelt too long or was hurried too fast, the exquisite faded beauty of Madam Bellamy, the noble dignity and manliness of the old planter and soldier, the perfect absence of reproach for others or whining pity for themselves, made the knowledge of their regret and loss doubly poignant. Their four sons had all laid down their lives in what they believed from their hearts to be their country's service; their daughters had died early, one from sorrow at her husband's death, and one from exposure in a forced flight across country; their ancestral home lay in ruins; their beloved cause had been put to shame and defeat — yet they could bow their heads to every blast of misfortune, and could make a man welcome at their table whose every instinct and tradition of loyalty made him their enemy. The owls might shriek from the chimneys of Fairford, and the timid wild hares course up and down the weed-grown avenues on an autumn night like this, but a welcome from the Bellamys was a welcome still. It seemed to the young imaginative guest that the old motto of the house was never so full of significance as when he fancied it exchanged between the Colonel and himself, Southerner and Northerner, elder and younger man, conquered and conqueror in an unhappy war. The two old portraits, with their warped frames and bullet-holes, faded and gleamed again in the firelight; the portrait of an elderly man was like the Colonel himself, but the woman, who was younger, and who seemed to meet Tom's eye gayly enough, bore a resemblance which he could only half recall. It was very late when the two men said good-night. They were each conscious of the great delight of having found a friend. The candles had flickered out long before, but the fire still burned, and struck a ray of light from the cup on the table.

VII

The next morning Burton waked early in his tiny sleeping-room. The fragrance of ripe grapes and the autumn air blew in at the window, and he hastened to dress, especially as he could hear the footstep and imperious voice of Colonel Bellamy, who seemed to begin his new day with zest and courage in the outer room. Milton, the old gray-headed negro, was there too, and was alternately upbraided and spoken with most intimately and with friendly approval. It sounded for a time as if some great excitement and project were on foot; but Milton presently appeared, eager for morning offices, and when Tom went out to join the Colonel he was no longer there. There were no signs of breakfast. The birds were singing in the trees outside, and the sun shone in through the wide-opened door. It was a poor place in the morning light. As he crossed the room he saw an old-fashioned gift-book lying on the couch, as if some one had just laid it there face downward. He carried it with him to the door; a dull collection enough, from forgotten writers of forgotten prose and verse, but the Colonel had left it open at some lines which, with all their faults, could not be read without sympathy. He was always thinking of his wife; he had marked the four verses because they spoke of her.

Tom put the old book down just as Colonel Bellamy passed outside, and hastened to join him. They met with pleasure, and stood together talking. The elder man presently quoted a line or two of poetry about the beauty of the autumn morning, and his companion stood listening with respectful attention, but he observed by contrast the hard, warrior-like lines of the Colonel's face. He could well believe that, until sorrow had softened him, a fiery impatient temper had ruled this Southern heart. There was a sudden chatter and noise of voices, and they both turned to see a group of negroes, small and great, coming across the lawn with bags and baskets, and after a few muttered words the old master set forth hurriedly to meet them, Tom following.

"Be still, all of you!" said the Colonel sternly. "Your mistress is still asleep. Go round to Milton, and he will attend to you. I'll come presently."

They were almost all old people, many of them were already infirm, and it was hard to still their requests and complaints. One of the smaller children clasped Colonel Bellamy about the knees. There was something patriarchal in the scene, and one could not help being sure that some reason for the present poverty of Fairford was the necessity for protecting these poor souls. The merry, well-fed colored people, who were indulging their late-won liberty of travel on the trains, had evidently shirked any responsibilities for such stray remnants of humanity. Slavery was its own provider for old age. There had once been no necessity for the slaves themselves to make provision for winter, as even a squirrel must. They were worse than children now, and far more appealing in their helplessness.

The group slowly departed, and Colonel Bellamy led the way in the opposite direction, toward the ruins of the great house. They crossed the old garden, where some ancient espaliers still clung to the broken brick-work of the walls, and a little fruit still clung to the knotted branches, while great hedges of box, ragged and uncared for, traced the old order of the walks. The heavy dew and warm morning sun brought out that antique fragrance,—the faint pungent odor which wakes the utmost memories of the past. Tom Burton thought with a sudden thrill that the girl with the sweet eyes yesterday had worn a bit of box in her dress. Here and there, under the straying boughs of the shrubbery, bloomed a late scarlet poppy from some scattered seed of which such old soil might well be full. It was a barren, neglected garden enough, but still full of charm and delight, being a garden. There was a fine fragrance of grapes through the undergrowth, but the whole place was completely ruined; a little snake slid from the broken base of a sun-dial, the tall chimneys of the house were already beginning to crumble, and birds and squirrels lived in their crevices and flitted about their lofty tops. At some distance an old negro was singing, — it must have been Milton himself, still unbesought by his dependents, — and the song was full of strange, monotonous wails and plaintive cadences, like a lament for war itself, and all the misery that follows in its train.

Colonel Bellamy had not spoken for some moments, but when they reached the terrace which had been before the house there were two flights of stone steps that led to empty air, and these were still adorned by some graceful railings and balusters, bent and rusty and broken.

"You will observe this iron-work, sir," said the Colonel, stopping to regard with pride almost the only relic of the former beauty and state of Fairford. "My grandfather had the pattern carefully planned in Charleston, where such work was formerly well done by Frenchmen." He stopped to point out certain charming features of the design with his walking-stick, and then went on without a glance at the decaying chimneys or the weed-grown cellars and heaps of stones beneath.

The lovely October morning was more than half gone when Milton brought the horse round to the door, and the moment came to say farewell. The Colonel had shown sincere eagerness that the visit should be prolonged for at least another day, but a reason for hurry which the young man hardly confessed to himself was urging him back along the way he had come. He was ready to forget his plans for shooting and wandering eastward on the river shore. He had paid a parting visit to Madam Bellamy in her own room, where she lay on a couch in the sunshine, and had seen the silver cup — a lucky cup he devoutly hoped it might indeed be — on a light stand by her side. It held a few small flowers, as if it had so been brought in to her in the early morning. Her eyes were dim with weeping. She had not thought of its age and history, neither did the sight of such pathetic loot wake bitter feelings against her foes. It was only the cup that her little children had used, one after another, in their babyhood; the last and dearest had kept it longest, and even he was dead — fallen in battle, like the rest.

She wore a hood and wrapping of black lace, which brought out the delicacy of her features like some quaint setting. Her hand trembled as she bade her young guest farewell. As he looked back from the doorway she was like some exiled queen in a peasant's lodging, such dignity and sweet patience were in her look. "I think you bring good fortune," she said. "Nothing can make me so happy as to have my husband find a little pleasure."

As the young man crossed the outer room the familiar eyes of the old portrait caught his own with wistful insistency. He suddenly suspected the double reason: he had been dreaming of other eyes, and knew that his fellow-traveler had kept him company. "Madam Bellamy," he said, turning back, and blushing as he bent to speak to her in a lower voice, — "the portrait; is it like any one? is it like your granddaughter? Could I have seen her on my way here?"

Madam Bellamy looked up at his eager face with a light of unwonted pleasure in her eyes. "Yes," said she, "my granddaughter would have been on her way to Whitfields. She has always been thought extremely like the picture: it is her great-grandmother. Goodby; pray let us see you at Fairford again"; and they said farewell once more, while Tom Burton promised something, half to himself, about the Christmas hunt.

"*Je vous en prie
Belle amie,*"

he whispered, and a most lovely hope was in his heart.

"You have been most welcome," said the Colonel at parting. "I beg that you will be so kind as to repeat this visit. I shall hope that we may have some shooting together."

"I shall hope so too," answered Tom Burton, warmly. Then, acting from sudden impulse, he quickly unslung his gun, and begged his old friend to keep it — to use it, at any rate, until he came again.

The old Virginian did not reply for a moment. "Your grandfather would have done this, sir. I loved him, and I take it from you both. My own gun is too poor a thing to offer in return." His voice shook; it was the only approach to a lament, to a complaint, that he had made.

This was the moment of farewell; the young man held the Colonel's hand in a boyish eager grasp. "I wish that I might be like a son to you," he said. "May I write, sometimes, and may I really come to Fairford again?"

The old Colonel answered him most affectionately. "Oh, yes; we must think of the Christmas hunt," he said, and so they parted.

Tom Burton rode slowly away, and presently the fireless chimneys of Fairford were lost to sight behind the clustering trees. The noonday light was shining on the distant river; the road was untraveled and untenanted for miles together, except by the Northern rider and his Southern steed.

QUESTIONS AND SUGGESTIONS

1. "There was a tinge of autumn color on even the English elms as Tom Burton walked slowly up Beacon Street." Why on *even* the elms? If you do not know the difference between the English and the American elm, be on the lookout for the two. Each is so beautiful in its own way, — the American elm in its grace, the English elm in its sturdy strength — that one appreciates each more because of knowing the other.

2. What are the ways in which Miss Jewett gives you an impression of the position, wealth, and leisure of the Burtons in the opening section of the story, without deliberately talking of those things?

3. What special interest of Tom's — other than travel — is mentioned, which shows you that he was not a mere idler?

4. In what two ways did Tom and his grandmother interpret the motto? Can you suggest any other meaning?

5. The date of Tom's journey to Virginia seems to the editor to have been about 1878. Does it seem either earlier or later to you? Why?

6. What was the element of pathos, "the inmost secret," that Tom felt at once upon seeing the young Southern lady on the train?

7. When did you begin to suspect that the young lady belonged to the Bellamy household? When did you feel sure?

8. How do you account for the slight hesitation which both Colonel and Madam Bellamy showed at first in greeting Tom?

9. Find any expression describing Madam Bellamy which impressed you particularly.

10. "A woman who is charming in youth is still more charming in age to a man of Tom Burton's imagination." Why should she be?

A WAR DEBT

11. Find and read aloud an instance of Tom's good breeding; of the Colonel's; of Madam Bellamy's. Some of the instances of good breeding of which the story is so full are matters of custom and are due to social training; others are spontaneous expressions of kind-hearted consideration for others; find an illustration of each.

12. Find and read some of the passages in which Miss Jewett makes you feel the desolating effects of the war in the South.

13. Explain how this story might be regarded as a sermon against war.

14. Find in the story two significant statements about slavery.

15. Read the sentence which sums up what the Civil War had meant to the Bellamys. What else does the sentence tell you about them?

16. What constituted one steady drain upon their slender means after the war? What does it show you about them?

17. Find some little touch which shows that the Bellamys kept in their more straitened way of living some of the dignified customs of their prosperity.

18. Do you know or can you find out to what story by the great English novelist Thackeray, Colonel Bellamy referred in his talk with Tom?

19. "It was like the dread of going into battle, but the moment had come." To what moment does this refer and why was it so hard a moment?

20. What shows how dear a possession the cup had been to Colonel Bellamy? Why had it been especially precious to Madam Bellamy?

21. In giving the motto as Tom quoted it to himself just before leaving Fairford, the writer spells two of the words differently. Find out what the difference in spelling means.

22. What makes you sure that the "most lovely hope" was realized? You may be interested to know that when Miss Jewett first published the story, there was a little para-

graph in italics at the end, which ran as follows: "This was the way that, many years ago, a Northerner found his love, a poor but noble lady in the South, and Fortune smiled again upon the ruined house of Fairford." But the two paragraphs preceding the last paragraph in the story as you know it were omitted. Which of the two ways of ending the story do you prefer?

MISS ESTHER'S GUEST

The story of "Miss Esther's Guest" occurs in one of the later volumes, *A Native of Winby and Other Tales*. You would especially enjoy the story which gives the title to the volume, and also "Decoration Day" and "The Flight of Betsey Lane." A very true and touching story is that called "The Failure of David Berry." David Berry, unpretentious and honest, the victim of a "smarter" man, was a moral hero. In three of the remaining stories Miss Jewett writes of other than native New England people, and with the same delightful sympathy. Indeed there is not a story in the whole book that boys and girls could not understand and enjoy.

I

OLD Miss Porley put on her silk shawl, and arranged it carefully over her thin shoulders, and pinned it with a hand that shook a little as if she were much excited. She bent forward to examine the shawl in the mahogany-framed mirror, for there was a frayed and tender spot in the silk where she had pinned it so many years. The shawl was very old; it had been her mother's, and she disliked to wear it too often, but she never could make up her mind to go out into the street in summer, as some of her neighbors did, with nothing over her shoulders at all. Next she put on her bonnet and tried to set it straight, allowing for a wave in the looking-glass that made one side of her face appear much longer than the other; then she drew on a pair of well-darned silk gloves; one had a wide crack all the way up the back of the hand, but they were still neat and decent for every-day wear, if she were careful to keep her left hand under the edge of the shawl. She had discussed the propriety of drawing the raveled silk together, but a thick seam would look very ugly, and there was something accidental about the crack.

Then, after hesitating a few moments, she took a small piece of folded white letter-paper from the table and went out of the house, locking the door and trying it, and stepped away bravely down the village street. Everybody said, "How do you do, Miss Porley?" or "Good-mornin', Esther." Every one in Daleham knew the good woman; she was one of the unchanging persons, always to be found in her place, and always pleased and friendly and ready to take an interest in old and young. She and her mother, who had early been left a widow, had been for many years the village tailoresses and makers of little boys' clothes. Mrs. Porley had been dead three years, however, and her daughter "Easter," as old friends called our heroine, had lived quite alone. She was made very sorrowful by her loneliness, but she never could be persuaded to take anybody to board: she could not bear to think of any one's taking her mother's place.

It was a warm summer morning, and Miss Porley had not very far to walk, but she was still more shaky and excited by the time she reached the First Church parsonage. She stood at the gate undecidedly, and, after she pushed it open a little way, she drew back again, and felt a curious beating at her heart and a general reluctance of mind and body. At that moment the minister's wife, a pleasant young woman with a smiling, eager face, looked out of the window and asked the tremulous visitor to come in. Miss Esther straightened herself and went briskly up the walk; she was very fond of the minister's wife, who had only been in Daleham a few months.

"Won't you take off your shawl?" asked Mrs. Wayton affectionately; "I have just been making gingerbread, and you shall have a piece as soon as it cools."

"I don't know 's I ought to stop," answered Miss Esther, flushing quickly. "I came on business; I won't keep you long."

"Oh, please stay a little while," urged the hostess. "I'll take my sewing, if you don't mind; there are two or three things that I want to ask you about."

"I've thought and flustered a sight over taking this step," said good old Esther abruptly. "I had to conquer a sight o' reluctance, I must say. I've got so used to livin' by myself that I sha'n't know how to consider another. But I see I ain't got common feelin' for others unless I can set my own comfort aside once in a while. I've brought you my name as one of those that will take one o' them city folks that needs a spell o' change. It come straight home to me how I should be feeling it by this time, if my lot had been cast in one o' them city garrets that the minister described so affecting. If 't had n't been for kind consideration somewheres, mother an' me might have sewed all them pleasant years away in the city that we enjoyed so in our own home, and our garding to step right out into when our sides set in to ache. And I ain't rich, but we was able to save a little something, and now I'm eatin' of it all up alone. It come to me I should like to have somebody take a taste out o' mother's part. Now, don't you let 'em send me no rampin' boys like them Barnard's folks had come last year, that vexed dumb creatur's so; and I don't know how to cope with no kind o' men-folks or strange girls, but I should know how to do for a woman that's getting well along in years, an' has come to feel kind o' spent. P'raps we ain't no right to pick an' choose, but I should know best how to make that sort comfortable on 'count of doin' for mother and studying what she preferred."

Miss Esther rose with quaint formality and put the folded paper, on which she had neatly written her name and address, into Mrs. Wayton's hand. Mrs. Wayton rose soberly to receive it, and then they both sat down again.

"I'm sure that you will feel more than repaid for your kindness, dear Miss Esther," said the minister's wife. "I know one of the ladies who have charge of the arrangements for the Country Week, and I will explain as well as I can the kind of guest you have in mind. I quite envy her: I have often thought, when I was busy and tired, how much I should like to run along the street and make you a visit in your dear old-fashioned little house."

"I should be more than pleased to have you, I'm sure," said Miss Esther, startled into a bright smile and forgetting her anxiety. "Come any day, and take me just as I am. We used to have a good deal o' company years ago, when there was a number o' mother's folks still livin' over Ashfield way. Sure as we had a pile o' work on hand and was hurrying for dear life an' limb, a wagon-load would light down at the front gate to spend the day an' have an early tea. Mother never was one to get flustered same's I do 'bout everything. She was a lovely cook, and she'd fill 'em up an' cheer 'em, and git 'em off early as she could, an' then we'd be kind o' waked up an' spirited ourselves, and would set up late sewin' and talkin' the company over, an' I'd have things saved to tell her that had been said while she was out o' the room. I make such a towse over everything myself, but mother was waked right up and felt pleased an' smart, if anything unexpected happened. I miss her more every year," and Miss Esther gave a great sigh. "I s'pose 't wa'n't reasonable to expect that I could have her to help me through with old age, but I'm a poor tool alone."

"Oh, no, you must n't say that!" exclaimed the minister's wife. "Why, nobody could get along without you. I wish I had come to Daleham in time to know your mother too."

Miss Esther shook her head sadly. "She would have set everything by you and Mr. Wayton. Now I must be getting back in case I'm wanted, but you let 'em send me somebody right away, while my bush beans is so nice. An' if any o' your little boy's clothes wants repairin', just give 'em to me; 't will be a real pleasant thing to set a few stitches. Or the minister's; ain't there something needed for him?"

Mrs. Wayton was about to say no, when she became conscious of the pleading old face before her. "I'm sure you are most kind, dear friend," she answered, "and I do have a great deal to do. I'll bring you two or three things to-night that are beyond my art, as I go to evening meeting. Mr. Wayton frayed out his best coat sleeve yesterday, and I was disheartened, for we had counted upon his not having a new one before the fall."

"'T would be mere play to me," said Miss Esther, and presently she went smiling down the street.

II

The Committee for the Country Week in a certain ward of Boston were considering the long list of children, and mothers with babies, and sewing-women, who were looking forward, some of them for the first time in many years, to a country holiday. Some were to go as guests to hospitable, generous farmhouses that opened their doors willingly now and then to tired city people; for some persons board could be paid.

The immediate arrangements of that time were settled at last, except that Mrs. Belton, the chairman, suddenly took a letter from her pocket. "I had almost forgotten this," she said; "it is another place offered in dear quiet old Daleham. My friend, the minister's wife there, writes me a word about it: 'The applicant desires especially an old person, being used to the care of an aged parent and sure of her power of making such a one comfortable, and she would like to have her guest come as soon as possible.' My friend asks me to choose a person of some refinement, — 'one who would appreciate the delicate simplicity and quaint ways of the hostess.'"

Mrs. Belton glanced hurriedly down the page. "I believe that's all," she said. "How about that nice old sewing-woman, Mrs. Connolly, in Bantry Street?"

"Oh, no!" some one entreated, looking up from her writing. "Why is n't it just the place for my old Mr. Rill, the dear old Englishman who lives alone up four flights in Town Court and has the bullfinch. He used to engrave seals, and his eyes gave out, and he is so thrifty with his own bit of savings and an atom of a pension. Some one pays his expenses to the country, and this sounds like a place he would be sure to like. I've been watching for the right chance."

"Take it, then," said the busy chairman, and there was a little more writing and talking, and then the committee meeting was over which settled Miss Esther Porley's fate.

III

The journey to Daleham was a great experience to Mr. Rill. He was a sensible old person, who knew well that he was getting stiffer and clumsier than need be in his garret, and that, as certain friends had said, a short time spent in the country would cheer and invigorate him. There had been occasional propositions that he should leave his garret altogether and go to the country to live, or at least to the suburbs of the city. He could not see things close at hand so well as he could take a wide outlook, and as his outlook from the one garret window was a still higher brick wall and many chimneys, he was losing a great deal that he might have had. But so long as he was expected to take an interest in the unseen and unknown he failed to accede to any plans about the country home, and declared that he was well enough in his high abode. He had lost a sister a few years before who had been his mainstay, but with his hands so well used to delicate work he had been less bungling in his simple household affairs than many another man might have been. But he was very lonely and was growing anxious; as he was rattled along in the train toward Daleham he held the chirping bullfinch's cage fast with both hands, and said to himself now and then, "This may lead to something; the country air smells very good to me."

The Daleham station was not very far out of the village, so that Miss Esther Porley put on her silk shawl and bonnet and everyday gloves just before four o'clock that afternoon, and went to meet her Country Week guest. Word had come the day before that the person for Miss Porley's would start two days in advance of the little company of children and helpless women, and since this message had come from the parsonage Miss Esther had worked diligently, late and early, to have her house in proper order. Whatever her mother had liked was thought of and provided. There were going to be rye shortcakes for tea, and there were some sprigs of thyme and sweet-balm in an old-fashioned wine-glass on the keeping-room table; mother always said they were so freshening. And Miss Esther had taken out a little shoulder-shawl and folded it over the arm of the rocking-chair by the window that looked out into the small garden where the London-pride was in full bloom, and the morning-glories had just begun to climb. Miss Esther was sixty-four herself, but still looked upon age as well in the distance.

She was always a prompt person, and had some minutes to wait at the station; then the time passed and the train was late. At last she saw the smoke far in the distance, and her heart began to sink. Perhaps she would not find it easy to get on with the old lady, and — well it was only for a week, and she had thought it right and best to take such a step, and now it would soon be over.

The train stopped, and there was no old lady at all.

Miss Esther had stood far back to get away from the smoke and roar, — she was always as afraid of the cars as she could be, — but as they moved away she took a few steps forward to scan the platform. There was no black bonnet with a worn lace veil, and no old lady with a burden of bundles; there were only the station master and two or three men, and an idle boy or two, and one cleanfaced, bent old man with a birdcage in one hand and an old carpet-bag in the other. She thought of the rye short-cakes for supper and all that she had done to make her small home pleasant, and her fire of excitement suddenly fell into ashes.

The old man with the bird-cage suddenly turned toward her. "Can you direct me to Miss Esther Porley's?" said he.

"I can," replied Miss Esther, looking at him with curiosity.

"I was directed to her house," said the pleasant old fellow, "by Mrs. Belton, of the Country Week Committee. My eyesight is poor. I should be glad if anybody would help me to find the place."

"You step this way with me, sir," said Miss Esther. She was afraid that the men on the platform heard every word they said, but nobody took particular notice, and off they walked down the road together. Miss Esther was enraged with the Country Week Committee.

"*You* were sent to — Miss Porley's?" she asked grimly, turning to look at him.

"I was, indeed," said Mr. Rill.

"I am Miss Porley, and I expected an old lady," she managed to say, and they both stopped and looked at each other with apprehension.

"I do declare!" faltered the old seal-cutter anxiously. "What had I better do, ma'am? They most certain give me your name. Maybe you could recommend me somewheres else, an' I can get home to-morrow if 't ain't convenient."

They were standing under a willow-tree in the shade; Mr. Rill took off his heavy hat, — it was a silk hat of by-gone shape; a golden robin began to sing, high in the willow, and the old bullfinch twittered and chirped in the cage. Miss Esther heard some footsteps coming behind them along the road. She changed color; she tried to remember that she was a woman of mature years and considerable experience.

"'T ain't a mite o' matter, sir," she said cheerfully. "I guess you'll find everything comfortable for you"; and they turned, much relieved, and walked along together.

"That's Lawyer Barstow's house," she said calmly, a minute afterward, "the handsomest place in town, we think 't is," and Mr. Rill answered politely that Daleham was a pretty place; he had not been out of the city for so many years that everything looked beautiful as a picture.

IV

Miss Porley rapidly recovered her composure, and bent her energies to the preparing of an early tea. She showed her guest to the snug bedroom under the low gambrel roof, and when she apologized for his having to go upstairs, he begged her to remember that it was nothing but a step to a man who was used to four long flights. They were both excited at finding a proper nail for the bird-cage outside the window, though Miss Esther said that she should love to have the pretty bird downstairs where they could see it and hear it sing. She said to herself over and over that if she could have her long-lost brother come home from sea, she should like to have him look and behave as gentle and kind as Mr. Rill. Somehow she found herself singing a cheerful hymn as she mixed and stirred the short-cakes. She could not help wishing that her mother were there to enjoy this surprise, but it did seem very odd, after so many years, to have a man in the house. It had not happened for fifteen years, at least, when they had entertained Deacon Sparks and wife, delegates from the neighboring town of East Wilby to the County Conference.

The neighbors did not laugh at Miss Esther openly or cause her to blush with self-consciousness, however much they may have discussed the situation and smiled behind her back. She took the presence of her guest with delighted simplicity, and the country week was extended to a fortnight, and then to a month. At last, one day Miss Esther and Mr. Rill were seen on their way to the railroad station, with a large bundle apiece beside the carpet-bag, though some one noticed that the bullfinch was left behind. Miss Esther came back alone, looking very woebegone and lonely, and if the truth must be known, she found her house too solitary. She looked into the woodhouse, where there was a great store of kindlings, neatly piled, and her water-pail was filled to the brim, her garden-paths were clean of weeds and swept, and yet everywhere she looked it seemed more lonely than ever. She pinned on her shawl again and went along the street to the parsonage.

"My old lady's just gone," she said to the minister's wife. "I was so lonesome I could not stay in the house."

"You found him a very pleasant visitor, did n't you, Miss Esther?" asked Mrs. Wayton, laughing a little.

"I did so; he wa'n't like other men, — kind and friendly and fatherly, and never stayed round when I was occupied, but entertained himself down street considerable, an' was as industrious as a bee, always asking me if there wa'n't something he could do about house. He and a sister some years older used to keep house together, and it was her long sickness used up what they 'd saved, and yet he 's got a little somethin', and there are friends he used to work for, jewelers, a big firm, that gives him somethin' regular. He 's goin' to see," — and Miss Esther blushed crimson, — "he 's goin' to see if they 'd be willin' to pay it just the same if he come to reside in Daleham. He thinks the air agrees with him here."

"Does he indeed?" inquired the minister's wife, with deep interest and a look of amusement.

"Yes 'm," said Miss Esther simply; "but don't you go an' say nothin' yet. I don't want folks to make a joke of it. Seems to me if he does feel to come back, and remains of the same mind he went away, we might be judicious to take the step" —

"Why, Miss Esther!" exclaimed the listener.

"Not till fall, — not till fall," said Miss Esther hastily. "I ain't going to count on it too much anyway. I expect we could get along; there's considerable goodness left in me, and you can always work better when you've got somebody beside yourself to work for. There, now I've told you I feel as if I was blown away in a gale."

"Why, I don't know what to say at such a piece of news!" exclaimed Mrs. Wayton again.

"I don't know 's there 's anything *to* say," gravely answered Miss Esther. "But I did laugh just now coming in the gate to think what a twitter I got into the day I fetched you that piece of paper."

"Why, I must go right and tell Mr. Wayton!" said the minister's wife.

"Oh, don't you, Mis' Wayton; no, no!" begged Miss Esther, looking quite coy and girlish. "I really don't know 's it 's quite settled, — it don't seem 's if it could be. I 'm going to hear from him in the course of a week. But I suppose *he* thinks it 's settled; he 's left the bird."

QUESTIONS AND SUGGESTIONS

1. How does Miss Jewett make you realize the old-fashioned quality and the straitened circumstances of Miss Esther in the very first paragraph?

2. What sort of house did Miss Esther live in? In what two places are you told about it?

3. What was Miss Esther's objection to the boys who had been at the Barnards' the year before? What does this strong objection tell you about her?

4. Why did Miss Esther hesitate so long about offering to take a "Country Week" guest?

5. Tell all you can about Miss Esther's mother. Should you have liked her? Why? What other member of the family is mentioned?

6. What must Mrs. Belton have overlooked in reading her letter from Mrs. Wayton?

7. How did Mr. Rill busy himself while he was at Miss Esther's?

8. What curious word is used for sitting-room?

9. What do you think is the most amusing place in the story?

MARTHA'S LADY

"Martha's Lady" is to be found in the same volume with "The Night before Thanksgiving." (See introductory note to that story.) It is pleasant to know that this story was peculiarly dear to Miss Jewett herself. She spoke of it as one into which she had put much time and thought and affection; and in a letter to some one who dearly loved the story, she once wrote, "It went to my heart to find such a friend of Martha's Lady."

In one of Miss Jewett's loveliest stories, "The Life of Nancy," Nancy says, "There's nothing so beautiful to me as manners." I sometimes wonder if that may not have been a true expression of Miss Jewett's own feeling, for the people whom one loves best in her stories — from Kate Lancaster with her perfect good breeding, and Madam Bellamy looking "like some exiled queen in a peasant's lodging," to dear Nancy Gale in her narrow village environment and that most exquisite of hostesses, Mrs. Blackett,[1] on her lonely island — all attract us by their manners, manners which are plainly the expression of sincere, generous, and gentle natures. And Miss Jewett's stories show us not only the beauty of genuine good manners but their infectiousness. This we feel strongly in "Martha's Lady." But we feel much more than this, — we feel the abiding reality of a deep and grateful affection, expressing itself in service, triumphing over time and change and absence, transfiguring life.

It might be wise for the teacher to read aloud certain of the more difficult paragraphs, such as the fourth, giving a free translation where the wording is especially difficult.

[1] Mrs. Blackett is in "The Country of the Pointed Firs."

This is an interesting and effective way of enlarging the pupil's vocabulary, and it prevents a story that ought to be a pleasure from becoming a burden.

I

ONE day, many years ago, the old Judge Pyne house wore an unwonted look of gayety and youthfulness. The high-fenced green garden was bright with June flowers. Under the elms in the large shady front yard you might see some chairs placed near together, as they often used to be when the family were all at home and life was going on gayly with eager talk and pleasure-making; when the elder judge, the grandfather, used to quote that great author, Dr. Johnson, and say to his girls, "Be brisk, be splendid, and be public."

One of the chairs had a crimson silk shawl thrown carelessly over its straight back, and a passer-by, who looked in through the latticed gate between the tall gate posts with their white urns, might think that this piece of shining East Indian color was a huge red lily that had suddenly bloomed against the syringa bush. There were certain windows thrown wide open that were usually shut, and their curtains were blowing free in the light wind of a summer afternoon; it looked as if a large household had returned to the old house to fill the prim best rooms and find them full of cheer.

It was evident to every one in town that Miss Harriet Pyne, to use the village phrase, had company. She was the last of her family, and was by no means old; but being the last, and wonted to live with people much older than herself, she had formed all the habits of a serious elderly person. Ladies of her age, something past thirty, often wore discreet caps in those days, especially if they were married, but being single, Miss Harriet clung to youth in this respect, making the one concession of keeping her waving chestnut hair as smooth and stiffly arranged as possible. She had been the dutiful companion of her father and mother in their latest years, all her elder brothers and sisters having married and gone, or died and gone, out of the old house. Now that she was left alone it seemed quite the best thing frankly to accept the fact of age, and to turn more resolutely than ever to the companionship of duty and serious books. She was more serious and given to routine than her elders themselves, as sometimes happened when the daughters of New England gentlefolks were brought up wholly in the society of their elders. At thirty-five she had more reluctance than her mother to face an unforeseen occasion, certainly more than her grandmother, who had preserved some cheerful inheritance of gayety and worldliness from colonial times.

There was something about the look of the crimson silk shawl in the front yard to make one suspect that the sober customs of the best house in a quiet New England village were all being set at defiance, and once when the mistress of the house came to stand in her own doorway, she wore the pleased but somewhat apprehensive look of a guest. In those days New England life held the necessity of much dignity and discretion of behavior; there was the truest hospitality and good cheer in all occasional festivities, but it was sometimes a self-conscious hospitality, followed by an inexorable return to asceticism both of diet and of behavior. Miss Harriet Pyne belonged to the very dullest days of New England, those which perhaps held the most priggishness for the learned professions, the most limited interpretation of the word " evangelical," and the pettiest indifference to large things. The outbreak of a desire for larger religious freedom caused at first a most determined reaction toward formalism, especially in small and quiet villages like Ashford, intently busy with their own concerns. It was high time for a little leaven to begin its work, in this moment when the great impulses of the war for liberty had died away and those of the coming war for patriotism and a new freedom had hardly yet begun.

The dull interior, the changed life of the old house, whose former activities seemed to have fallen sound asleep, really typified these larger conditions, and a little leaven had made its easily recognized appearance in the shape of a light-hearted girl. She was Miss Harriet's young Boston cousin, Helena Vernon, who, half-amused and half-impatient at the unnecessary sober-mindedness of her hostess and of Ashford in general, had set herself to the difficult task of gayety. Cousin Harriet looked on at a succession of ingenious and, on the whole, innocent attempts at pleasure, as she might have looked on at the frolics of a kitten who easily substitutes a ball of yarn for the uncertainties of a bird or a wind-blown leaf, and who may at any moment ravel the fringe of a sacred curtain-tassel in preference to either.

Helena, with her mischievous appealing eyes, with her enchanting old songs and her guitar, seemed the more delightful and even reasonable because she was so kind to everybody, and because she was a beauty. She had the gift of most charming manners. There was all the unconscious lovely ease and grace that had come with the good breeding of her city home, where many pleasant people came and went; she had no fear, one had almost said no respect, of the individual, and she did not need to think of herself. Cousin Harriet turned cold with apprehension when she saw the minister coming in at the front gate, and wondered in agony if Martha were properly attired to go to the door, and would by any chance hear the knocker; it was Helena who, delighted to have anything happen, ran to the door to welcome the Reverend Mr. Crofton as if he were a congenial friend of her own age. She could behave with more or less propriety during the stately first visit, and even contrive to lighten it with modest mirth, and to extort the confession that the guest had a tenor voice, though sadly out of practice; but when the minister departed a little flattered, and hoping that he had not expressed himself too strongly for a pastor upon the poems of Emerson, and feeling the unusual stir of gallantry in his proper heart, it was Helena who caught the honored hat of the late Judge Pyne from its last resting-place in the hall, and holding it securely in both hands, mimicked the minister's self-conscious entrance. She copied his pompous and anxious expression in the dim parlor in such delicious fashion that Miss Harriet, who could not always extinguish a ready spark of the original sin of humor, laughed aloud.

"My dear!" she exclaimed severely the next moment, "I am ashamed of your being so disrespectful!" and then laughed again, and took the affecting old hat and carried it back to its place.

"I would not have had any one else see you for the world," she said sorrowfully as she returned, feeling quite self-possessed again, to the parlor doorway; but

Helena still sat in the minister's chair, with her small feet placed as his stiff boots had been, and a copy of his solemn expression before they came to speaking of Emerson and of the guitar. "I wish I had asked him if he would be so kind as to climb the cherry-tree," said Helena, unbending a little at the discovery that her cousin would consent to laugh no more. "There are all those ripe cherries on the top branches. I can climb as high as he, but I can't reach far enough from the last branch that will bear me. The minister is so long and thin!"

"I don't know what Mr. Crofton would have thought of you; he is a very serious young man," said cousin Harriet, still ashamed of her laughter. "Martha will get the cherries for you, or one of the men. I should not like to have Mr. Crofton think you were frivolous, a young lady of your opportunities" — but Helena had escaped through the hall and out at the garden door at the mention of Martha's name. Miss Harriet Pyne sighed anxiously, and then smiled, in spite of her deep convictions, as she shut the blinds and tried to make the house look solemn again.

The front door might be shut, but the garden door at the other end of the broad hall was wide open upon the large sunshiny garden, where the last of the red and white peonies and the golden lilies, and the first of the tall blue larkspurs lent their colors in generous fashion. The straight box borders were all in fresh and shining green of their new leaves, and there was a fragrance of the old garden's inmost life and soul blowing from the honeysuckle blossoms on a long trellis. It was now late in the afternoon, and the sun was low behind great apple-trees at the garden's end, which threw their shadows over the short turf of the bleaching-green. The cherry-trees stood at one side in full sunshine, and Miss Harriet, who presently came to the garden steps to watch like a hen at the water's edge, saw her cousin's pretty figure in its white dress of India muslin hurrying across the grass. She was accompanied by the tall, ungainly shape of Martha, the new maid, who, dull and indifferent to every one else, showed a surprising willingness and allegiance to the young guest.

"Martha ought to be in the dining-room, already, slow as she is; it wants but half an hour of tea-time," said Miss Harriet, as she turned and went into the shaded house. It was Martha's duty to wait at table, and there had been many trying scenes and defeated efforts toward her education. Martha was certainly very clumsy, and she seemed the clumsier because she had replaced her aunt, a most skillful person, who had but lately married a thriving farm and its prosperous owner. It must be confessed that Miss Harriet was a most bewildering instructor, and that her pupil's brain was easily confused and prone to blunders. The coming of Helena had been somewhat dreaded by reason of this incompetent service, but the guest took no notice of frowns or futile gestures at the first tea-table, except to establish friendly relations with Martha on her own account by a reassuring smile. They were about the same age, and next morning, before cousin Harriet came down, Helena showed by a word and a quick touch the right way to do something that had gone wrong and been impossible to understand the night before. A moment later the anxious mistress came in without suspicion, but Martha's eyes were as affectionate as a dog's, and there was a new look of hopefulness on her face; this dreaded guest was a friend after all, and not a foe come from proud Boston to confound her ignorance and patient efforts.

The two young creatures, mistress and maid, were hurrying across the bleaching-green.

"I can't reach the ripest cherries," explained Helena politely, "and I think that Miss Pyne ought to send some to the minister. He has just made us a call. Why, Martha, you have n't been crying again!"

"Yes 'm," said Martha sadly. "Miss Pyne always loves to send something to the minister," she acknowledged with interest, as if she did not wish to be asked to explain these latest tears.

"We'll arrange some of the best cherries in a pretty dish. I'll show you how, and you shall carry them over to the parsonage after tea," said Helena cheerfully, and Martha accepted the embassy with pleasure. Life was beginning to hold moments of something like delight in the last few days.

"You'll spoil your pretty dress, Miss Helena," Martha gave shy warning, and Miss Helena stood back and held up her skirts with unusual care while the country girl, in her heavy blue checked gingham, began to climb the cherry-tree like a boy.

Down came the scarlet fruit like bright rain into the green grass.

"Break some nice twigs with the cherries and leaves together; oh, you 're a duck, Martha!" and Martha, flushed with delight, and looking far more like a thin and solemn blue heron, came rustling down to earth again, and gathered the spoils into her clean apron.

That night at tea, during her handmaiden's temporary absence, Miss Harriet announced, as if by way of apology, that she thought Martha was beginning to understand something about her work. "Her aunt was a treasure, she never had to be told anything twice; but Martha has been as clumsy as a calf," said the precise mistress of the house. " I have been afraid sometimes that I never could teach her anything. I was quite ashamed to have you come just now, and find me so unprepared to entertain a visitor."

"Oh, Martha will learn fast enough because she cares so much," said the visitor eagerly. " I think she is a dear good girl. I do hope that she will never go away. I think she does things better every day, Cousin Harriet," added Helena pleadingly, with all her kind young heart. The china-closet door was open a little way, and Martha heard every word. From that moment, she not only knew what love was like, but she knew love's dear ambitions. To have come from a stony hill-farm and a bare small wooden house, was like a cave-dweller's coming to make a permanent home in an art museum, such had seemed the elaborateness and elegance of Miss Pyne's fashion of life; and Martha's simple brain was slow enough in its processes and recognitions. But with this sympathetic ally and defender, this exquisite Miss Helena who believed in her, all difficulties appeared to vanish.

Later that evening, no longer homesick or hopeless, Martha returned from her polite errand to the minister, and stood with a sort of triumph before the two ladies, who were sitting in the front doorway, as if they were waiting for visitors, Helena still in her white muslin and red ribbons, and Miss Harriet in a thin black silk. Being happily self-forgetful in the greatness of the moment, Martha's manners were perfect, and she looked for once almost pretty and quite as young as she was.

" The minister came to the door himself, and returned his thanks. He said that cherries were always his favorite fruit, and he was much obliged to both Miss Pyne and Miss Vernon. He kept me waiting a few minutes, while he got this book ready to send to you, Miss Helena."

"What are you saying, Martha? I have sent him nothing!" exclaimed Miss Pyne, much astonished. "What does she mean, Helena?"

"Only a few cherries," explained Helena. "I thought Mr. Crofton would like them after his afternoon of parish calls. Martha and I arranged them before tea, and I sent them with our compliments."

"Oh, I am very glad you did," said Miss Harriet, wondering, but much relieved. "I was afraid" —

"No, it was none of my mischief," answered Helena daringly. "I did not think that Martha would be ready to go so soon. I should have shown you how pretty they looked among their green leaves. We put them in one of your best white dishes with the openwork edge. Martha shall show you to-morrow; mamma always likes to have them so." Helena's fingers were busy with the hard knot of a parcel.

"See this, Cousin Harriet!" she announced proudly, as Martha disappeared round the corner of the house, beaming with the pleasures of adventure and success. "Look! the minister has sent me a book: Sermons on *what?* Sermons — it is so dark that I can't quite see."

"It must be his 'Sermons on the Seriousness of Life'; they are the only ones he has printed, I believe," said Miss Harriet, with much pleasure. "They are considered very fine discourses. He pays you a great compliment, my dear. I feared that he noticed your girlish levity."

"I behaved beautifully while he stayed," insisted

Helena. "Ministers are only men," but she blushed with pleasure. It was certainly something to receive a book from its author, and such a tribute made her of more value to the whole reverent household. The minister was not only a man, but a bachelor, and Helena was at the age that best loves conquest; it was at any rate comfortable to be reinstated in cousin Harriet's good graces.

"Do ask the kind gentleman to tea! He needs a little cheering up," begged the siren in India muslin, as she laid the shiny black volume of sermons on the stone doorstep with an air of approval, but as if they had quite finished their mission.

"Perhaps I shall, if Martha improves as much as she has within the last day or two," Miss Harriet promised hopefully. "It is something I always dread a little when I am all alone, but I think Mr. Crofton likes to come. He converses so elegantly."

II

These were the days of long visits, before affectionate friends thought it quite worth while to take a hundred miles' journey merely to dine or to pass a night in one another's houses. Helena lingered through the pleasant weeks of early summer, and departed unwillingly at last to join her family at the White Hills, where they had gone, like other households of high social station, to pass the month of August out of town. The happy-hearted young guest left many lamenting friends behind her, and promised each that she would come back again next year. She left the minister a rejected lover, as well as the preceptor of the academy, but with their pride unwounded, and it may have been with wider outlooks upon the world and a less narrow sympathy both for their own work in life and for their neighbors' work and hindrances. Even Miss Harriet Pyne herself had lost some of the unnecessary provincialism and prejudice which had begun to harden a naturally good and open mind and affectionate heart. She was conscious of feeling younger and more free, and not so lonely. Nobody had ever been so gay, so fascinating, or so kind as Helena, so full of social resource, so simple and undemanding in her friendliness. The light of her young life cast no shadow on either young or old companions, her pretty clothes never seemed to make other girls look dull or out of fashion. When she went away up the street in Miss Harriet's carriage to take the slow train toward Boston and the gayeties of the new Profile House, where her mother waited impatiently with a group of Southern friends, it seemed as if there would never be any more picnics or parties in Ashford, and as if society had nothing left to do but to grow old and get ready for winter.

Martha came into Miss Helena's bed-room that last morning, and it was easy to see that she had been crying; she looked just as she did in that first sad week of homesickness and despair. All for love's sake she had been learning to do many things, and to do them exactly right; her eyes had grown quick to see the smallest chance for personal service. Nobody could be more humble and devoted; she looked years older than Helena, and wore already a touching air of caretaking.

"You spoil me, you dear Martha!" said Helena from the bed. "I don't know what they will say at home, I am so spoiled."

Martha went on opening the blinds to let in the

brightness of the summer morning, but she did not speak.

"You are getting on splendidly, are n't you?" continued the little mistress. "You have tried so hard that you make me ashamed of myself. At first you crammed all the flowers together, and now you make them look beautiful. Last night Cousin Harriet was so pleased when the table was so charming, and I told her that you did everything yourself, every bit. Won't you keep the flowers fresh and pretty in the house until I come back? It's so much pleasanter for Miss Pyne, and you'll feed my little sparrows, won't you? They're growing so tame."

"Oh, yes, Miss Helena!" and Martha looked almost angry for a moment, then she burst into tears and covered her face with her apron. "I could n't understand a single thing when I first came. I never had been anywhere to see anything, and Miss Pyne frightened me when she talked. It was you made me think I could ever learn. I wanted to keep the place, 'count of mother and the little boys; we're dreadful hard pushed. Hepsy has been good in the kitchen; she said she ought to have patience with me, for she was awkward herself when she first came."

Helena laughed; she looked so pretty under the tasseled white curtains.

"I dare say Hepsy tells the truth," she said. "I wish you had told me about your mother. When I come again, some day we'll drive up country, as you call it, to see her. Martha! I wish you would think of me sometimes after I go away. Won't you promise?" and the bright young face suddenly grew grave. "I have hard times myself; I don't always learn things that I ought to learn, I don't always put things straight. I wish you would n't forget me ever, and would just believe in me. I think it does help more than anything."

"I won't forget," said Martha slowly. "I shall think of you every day." She spoke almost with indifference, as if she had been asked to dust a room, but she turned aside quickly and pulled the little mat under the hot-water jug quite out of its former straightness; then she hastened away down the long white entry, weeping as she went.

III

To lose out of sight the friend whom one has loved and lived to please is to lose joy out of life. But if love is true, there comes presently a higher joy of pleasing the ideal, that is to say, the perfect friend. The same old happiness is lifted to a higher level. As for Martha, the girl who stayed behind in Ashford, nobody's life could seem duller to those who could not understand; she was slow of step, and her eyes were almost always downcast as if intent upon incessant toil; but they startled you when she looked up, with their shining light. She was capable of the happiness of holding fast to a great sentiment, the ineffable satisfaction of trying to please one whom she truly loved. She never thought of trying to make other people pleased with herself; all she lived for was to do the best she could for others, and to conform to an ideal, which grew at last to be like a saint's vision, a heavenly figure painted upon the sky.

On Sunday afternoons in summer, Martha sat by the window of her chamber, a low-storied little room, which looked into the side yard and the great branches of an elm-tree. She never sat in the old wooden rocking-chair except on Sundays like this; it belonged to the day of rest and to happy meditation. She wore her plain black dress and a clean white apron, and held in her lap a little wooden box, with a brass ring on top for a handle. She was past sixty years of age and looked even older, but there was the same look on her face that it had sometimes worn in girlhood. She was the same Martha; her hands were old-looking and work-worn, but her face still shone. It seemed like yesterday that Helena Vernon had gone away, and it was more than forty years.

War and peace had brought their changes and great anxieties, the face of the earth was furrowed by floods and fire, the faces of mistress and maid were furrowed by smiles and tears, and in the sky the stars shone on as if nothing had happened. The village of Ashford added a few pages to its unexciting history, the minister preached, the people listened; now and then a funeral crept along the street, and now and then the bright face of a little child rose above the horizon of a family pew. Miss Harriet Pyne lived on in the large white house, which gained more and more distinction because it suffered no changes, save successive repaintings and a new railing about its stately roof. Miss Harriet herself had moved far beyond the uncertainties of an anxious youth. She had long ago made all her decisions, and settled all necessary questions; her scheme of life was as faultless as the miniature landscape of a Japanese garden, and as easily kept in order. The only important change she would ever be capable of making was the final change to another and a better world; and for that nature itself would gently provide, and her own innocent life.

Hardly any great social event had ruffled the easy current of life since Helena Vernon's marriage. To this Miss Pyne had gone, stately in appearance and carrying gifts of some old family silver which bore the Vernon crest, but not without some protest in her heart against the uncertainties of married life. Helena was so equal to a happy independence and even to the assistance of other lives grown strangely dependent upon her quick sympathies and instinctive decisions, that it was hard to let her sink her personality in the affairs of another. Yet a brilliant English match was not without its attractions to an old-fashioned gentlewoman like Miss Pyne, and Helena herself was amazingly happy; one day there had come a letter to Ashford, in which her very heart seemed to beat with love and self-forgetfulness, to tell cousin Harriet of such new happiness and high hope. "Tell Martha all that I say about my dear Jack," wrote the eager girl; "please show my letter to Martha, and tell her that I shall come home next summer and bring the handsomest and best man in the world to Ashford. I have told him all about the dear house and the dear garden; there never was such a lad to reach for cherries with his six-foot-two." Miss Pyne, wondering a little, gave the letter to Martha, who took it deliberately and as if she wondered too, and went away to read it slowly by herself. Martha cried over it, and felt a strange sense of loss and pain; it hurt her heart a little to read about the cherry-picking. Her idol seemed to be less her own since she had become the idol of a stranger. She never had taken such a letter in her hands before, but love at last prevailed, since Miss Helena was happy, and she kissed the last page where her name was written, feeling overbold, and laid the envelope on Miss Pyne's secretary without a word.

The most generous love cannot but long for reassurance, and Martha had the joy of being remembered. She was not forgotten when the day of the wedding drew near, but she never knew that Miss Helena had asked if Cousin Harriet would not bring Martha to town; she should like to have Martha there to see her married. " She would help about the flowers," wrote the happy girl; "I know she will like to come, and I'll ask mamma to plan to have some one take her all about Boston and make her have a pleasant time after the hurry of the great day is over."

Cousin Harriet thought it was very kind and exactly like Helena, but Martha would be out of her element; it was most imprudent and girlish to have thought of such a thing. Helena's mother would be far from wishing for any unnecessary guest just then, in the busiest part of her household, and it was best not to speak of the invitation. Some day Martha should go to Boston if she did well, but not now. Helena did not forget to ask if Martha had come, and was astonished by the indifference of the answer. It was the first thing which reminded her that she was not a fairy princess having everything her own way in that last day before the wedding. She knew that Martha would have loved to be near, for she could not help understanding in that moment of her own happiness the love that was hidden in another heart. Next day this happy young princess, the bride, cut a piece of a great cake and put it into a pretty box that had held one of her wedding presents. With eager voices calling her, and all her friends about her, and her mother's face growing more and more wistful at the thought of parting, she still lingered and ran to take one or two trifles from her dressing-table, a little mirror and some tiny scissors that Martha would remember, and one of the pretty handkerchiefs marked with her maiden name. These she put in the box too; it was half a girlish freak and fancy, but she could not help trying to share her happiness, and Martha's life was so plain and dull. She whispered a message, and put the little package into Cousin Harriet's hand for Martha as she said good-by. She was very fond of Cousin Harriet. She smiled with a gleam of her old fun; Martha's puzzled look and tall awkward figure seemed to stand suddenly before her eyes, as she promised to come again to Ashford. Impatient voices called to Helena, her lover was at the door, and she hurried away, leaving her old home and her girlhood gladly. If she had only known it, as she kissed Cousin Harriet good-by, they were never going to see each other again until they were old women. The first step that she took out of her father's house that day, married, and full of hope and joy, was a step that led her away from the green elms of Boston Common and away from her own country and those she loved best, to a brilliant, much-varied foreign life, and to nearly all the sorrows and nearly all the joys that the heart of one woman could hold or know.

On Sunday afternoons Martha used to sit by the window in Ashford and hold the wooden box which a favorite young brother, who afterward died at sea, had made for her, and she used to take out of it the pretty little box with a gilded cover that had held the piece of wedding-cake, and the small scissors, and the blurred bit of a mirror in its silver case; as for the handkerchief with the narrow lace edge, once in two or three years she sprinkled it as if it were a flower, and spread it out in the sun on the old bleaching-green, and sat near by in the shrubbery to watch lest some bold robin or cherry-bird should seize it and fly away.

IV

Miss Harriet Pyne was often congratulated upon the good fortune of having such a helper and friend as Martha. As time went on this tall, gaunt woman, always thin, always slow, gained a dignity of behavior and simple affectionateness of look which suited the charm and dignity of the ancient house. She was unconsciously beautiful like a saint, like the picturesqueness of a lonely tree which lives to shelter unnumbered lives and to stand quietly in its place. There was such rustic homeliness and constancy belonging to her, such beautiful powers of apprehension, such reticence, such gentleness for those who were troubled or sick; all these gifts and graces Martha hid in her heart. She never joined the church because she thought she was not good enough, but life was such a passion and happiness of service that it was impossible not to be devout, and she was always in her humble place on Sundays, in the back pew next the door. She had been educated by a remembrance; Helena's young eyes forever looked at her reassuringly from a gay girlish face. Helena's sweet patience in teaching her own awkwardness could never be forgotten.

"I owe everything to Miss Helena," said Martha, half aloud, as she sat alone by the window; she had said it to herself a thousand times. When she looked in the little keepsake mirror she always hoped to see some faint reflection of Helena Vernon, but there was only her own brown old New England face to look back at her wonderingly.

Miss Pyne went less and less often to pay visits to her friends in Boston; there were very few friends left to come to Ashford and make long visits in the summer, and life grew more and more monotonous. Now and then there came news from across the sea and messages of remembrance, letters that were closely written on thin sheets of paper, and that spoke of lords and ladies, of great journeys, of the death of little children and the proud successes of boys at school, of the wedding of Helena Dysart's only daughter; but even that had happened years ago. These things seemed far away and vague, as if they belonged to a story and not to life itself; the true links with the past were quite different. There was the unvarying flock of ground-sparrows that Helena had begun to feed; every morning Martha scattered crumbs for them from the side doorsteps while Miss Pyne watched from the dining-room window, and they were counted and cherished year by year.

Miss Pyne herself had many fixed habits, but little ideality or imagination, and so at last it was Martha who took thought for her mistress, and gave freedom to her own good taste. After a while, without any one's observing the change, the every-day ways of doing things in the house came to be the stately ways that had once belonged only to the entertainment of guests. Happily both mistress and maid seized all possible chances for hospitality, yet Miss Harriet nearly always sat alone at her exquisitely served table with its fresh flowers, and the beautiful old china which Martha handled so lovingly that there was no good excuse for keeping it hidden on closet shelves. Every year when the old cherry-trees were in fruit, Martha carried the round white old English dish with a fretwork edge, full of pointed green leaves and scarlet cherries, to the minister, and his wife never quite understood why every year he blushed and looked so conscious of the pleasure, and thanked Martha as if he had received a very particular attention. There was no pretty suggestion toward the pursuit of the fine art of housekeeping in Martha's limited acquaintance with newspapers that she did not adopt; there was no refined old custom of the Pyne housekeeping that she consented to let go. And every day, as she had promised, she thought of Miss Helena, — oh, many times in every day: whether this thing would please her, or that be likely to fall in with her fancy or ideas of fitness. As far as was possible the rare news that reached Ashford through an occasional letter or the talk of guests was made part of Martha's own life, the history of her own heart. A worn old geography often stood open at the map of Europe on the lightstand in her room, and a little old-fashioned gilt button, set with a bit of glass like a ruby, that had broken and fallen from the trimming of one of Helena's dresses, was used to mark the city of her dwelling-place. In the changes of a diplomatic life Martha followed her lady all about the map. Sometimes the button was at Paris, and sometimes at Madrid; once, to her great anxiety, it remained long at St. Petersburg. For such a slow scholar Martha was not unlearned at last, since everything about life in these foreign towns was of interest to her faithful heart. She satisfied her own mind as she threw crumbs to the tame sparrows; it was all part of the same thing and for the same affectionate reasons.

V

One Sunday afternoon in early summer Miss Harriet Pyne came hurrying along the entry that led to Martha's room and called two or three times before its inhabitant could reach the door. Miss Harriet looked unusually cheerful and excited, and she held something in her hand. "Where are you, Martha?" she called again. "Come quick, I have something to tell you!"

"Here I am, Miss Pyne," said Martha, who had only stopped to put her precious box in the drawer, and to shut the geography.

"Who do you think is coming this very night at half-past six? We must have everything as nice as we can; I must see Hannah at once. Do you remember my cousin Helena who has lived abroad so long? Miss Helena Vernon, — the Honorable Mrs. Dysart, she is now."

"Yes, I remember her," answered Martha, turning a little pale.

"I knew that she was in this country, and I had written to ask her to come for a long visit," continued Miss Harriet, who did not often explain things, even to Martha, though she was always conscientious about the kind messages that were sent back by grateful guests. "She telegraphs that she means to anticipate her visit by a few days and come to me at once. The heat is beginning in town, I suppose. I daresay, having been a foreigner so long, she does not mind traveling on Sunday. Do you think Hannah will be prepared? We must have tea a little later."

"Yes, Miss Harriet," said Martha. She wondered that she could speak as usual, there was such a ringing in her ears. "I shall have time to pick some fresh strawberries; Miss Helena is so fond of our strawberries."

"Why, I had forgotten," said Miss Pyne, a little puzzled by something quite unusual in Martha's face. "We must expect to find Mrs. Dysart a good deal changed, Martha; it is a great many years since she was here; I have not seen her since her wedding, and she has had a great deal of trouble, poor girl. You had better open the parlor chamber, and make it ready before you go down."

"It is all ready," said Martha. "I can carry some of those little sweet-brier roses upstairs before she comes."

"Yes, you are always thoughtful," said Miss Pyne, with unwonted feeling.

Martha did not answer. She glanced at the telegram wistfully. She had never really suspected before that Miss Pyne knew nothing of the love that had been in her heart all these years; it was half a pain and half a golden joy to keep such a secret; she could hardly bear this moment of surprise.

Presently the news gave wings to her willing feet. When Hannah, the cook, who never had known Miss Helena, went to the parlor an hour later on some errand to her old mistress, she discovered that this stranger guest must be a very important person. She had never seen the tea-table look exactly as it did that night, and in the parlor itself there were fresh blossoming boughs in the old East India jars, and lilies in the paneled hall, and flowers everywhere, as if there were some high festivity.

Miss Pyne sat by the window watching, in her best dress, looking stately and calm; she seldom went out now, and it was almost time for the carriage. Martha was just coming in from the garden with the strawberries, and with more flowers in her apron. It was a bright cool evening in June, the golden robins sang in the elms, and the sun was going down behind the apple-trees at the foot of the garden. The beautiful old house stood wide open to the long-expected guest.

"I think that I shall go down to the gate," said Miss Pyne, looking at Martha for approval, and Martha nodded and they went together slowly down the broad front walk.

There was a sound of horses and wheels on the roadside turf: Martha could not see at first; she stood back inside the gate behind the white lilac-bushes as the carriage came. Miss Pyne was there; she was holding out both arms and taking a tired, bent little figure in black to her heart. "Oh, my Miss Helena is an old woman like me!" and Martha gave a pitiful sob; she had never dreamed it would be like this; this was the one thing she could not bear.

"Where are you, Martha?" called Miss Pyne. "Martha will bring these in; you have not forgotten my good Martha, Helena?" Then Mrs. Dysart looked up and smiled just as she used to smile in the old days. The young eyes were there still in the changed face, and Miss Helena had come.

That night Martha waited in her lady's room just as she used, humble and silent, and went through with the old unforgotten loving services. The long years seemed like days. At last she lingered a moment trying to think of something else that might be done; then she was going silently away, but Helena called her back. She suddenly knew the whole story and could hardly speak.

"Oh, my dear Martha!" she cried, "won't you kiss me good-night? Oh, Martha, have you remembered like this, all these long years!"

QUESTIONS AND SUGGESTIONS

1. "One day, many years ago." At about what date does the story open?
2. Speak of two or three things which show that the story deals with a time many years past.
3. Stand a moment at the open front door of the old Judge Pyne house and tell what you see as you look out, and then as you look in.
4. Describe the garden as it looked in June.
5. Describe Helena as she appears at the opening of the story; at the end. In what respects was she unchanged?
6. Describe Martha's appearance at the beginning of the story; at the end. Was the change in her greater or less than in Helena?
7. Find and read the words that account for Helena's charm.
8. Tell what happened at the tea-table on the night of Helena's arrival.
9. Why was Helena more successful than Miss Harriet in teaching Martha to wait on table?
10. When did Martha first seem well-mannered and "almost pretty"? Why did she seem so?
11. Mention one very delightful thing that Helena taught Martha to do well.
12. Find and read the one short sentence in which Miss Jewett refers to Martha's aunt (p. 100). See how much she tells you about her in a few words and contrast her with Martha.
13. What helped Martha to be happy after Helena had gone away?
14. What proofs are there of Helena's continued interest in Martha after Helena went back to the city?

15. "The true links with the past were quite different." What were some of these links?

16. Read the lines on page 108 beginning "War and peace" and ending "a family pew." These lines have the force and beauty of poetry. Choose the picture that seems most vivid to you.

17. "She was always conscientious about the kind messages that were sent back by grateful guests." Whom does *she* mean? What does the passage tell you about Martha? About the guests?

18. When does Miss Pyne show unwonted appreciation of Martha? How does she express it?

19. Why had she never recognized Martha's deep feeling for Helena?

20. In what way did the customs of the house change during the forty years?

21. Tell all that the title of the story means to you. Would "Martha's Miss Helena" be an equally good name? Make a good name of your own for the story.

22. Mention some one incident that you would be very unwilling to have left out of the story. Why?

23. What incident in the story do you wish had happened differently?

24. Should you be as well satisfied to have the story end just before the last two paragraphs? Give your reasons.

25. Which of the three characters — the old-fashioned gentlewoman, the younger lady, or the faithful servant — do you care the most for, and why?

26. Find in Part IV a brief statement that expresses the meaning of the whole story in a few words.

BIRDS AND ANIMALS

BURROUGHS, JOHN
   Bird Stories from Burroughs. Illustrated. 60 cents, *net.*
   Squirrels and Other Fur-Bearers. Illustrated. *School Edition.* 60 cents, *net.*
   Afoot and Afloat. *Riverside Literature Series*, No. 176. Paper, 15 cents; cloth, 25 cents, *net.*
   Birds and Bees. *R. L. S.*, No. 28. Paper, 15 cents, *net.* Nos. 28 and 36 in one volume, cloth, 40 cents, *net.*
   Bunch of Herbs, and Other Papers. *R. L. S.*, No. 92. Paper, 15 cents, *net.*
   Sharp Eyes, and Other Papers. *R. L. S.*, No. 36. Paper, 15 cents; cloth, 25 cents, *net.*

MILLER, OLIVE THORNE
   True Bird Stories from my Note-Books. Illustrated. *School Edition.* 60 cents, *net.*
   The First Book of Birds. Illustrated. *School Edition.* 60 cents, *net.*
   The Second Book of Birds: Bird Families. Illustrated. $1.00, *net.*

SHARP, DALLAS LORE
   The Fall of the Year. Illustrated. 60 cents, *net.*

PLANTS

EASTMAN, HELEN
   New England Ferns and their Common Allies. Illustrated. $1.25, *net.*

SARGENT, FREDERICK LE ROY
   Corn Plants: Their Uses and Ways of Life. Illustrated. 75 cents.

THOREAU, HENRY D.
   Katahdin and Chesuncook. From "The Maine Woods." With an introduction. Illustrated. *Riverside Literature Series*, No. 186. Paper, 15 cents, *net;* linen, 25 cents, *net.*
   The Succession of Forest Trees, Wild Apples, and Sounds. *R. L. S.*, No. 27. Paper, 15 cents, *net.* Also in one volume with Burroughs' Birds and Bees (No. 28) and Warner's A-Hunting of the Deer (No. 37), cloth, 50 cents, *net.*
   Walden. Edited by Francis H. Allen. Illustrated. *R. L. S.*, No. 195. (*Triple Number.*) Paper, .45; cloth, .50.

HOUGHTON MIFFLIN COMPANY
BOSTON   NEW YORK   CHICAGO

The Dallas Lore Sharp Nature Series

I. THE FALL OF THE YEAR
II. WINTER
III. THE SPRING OF THE YEAR
IV. SUMMER

BY

DALLAS LORE SHARP

Author of "The Face of the Fields," "The Lay of the Land," etc.

Illustrated by ROBERT BRUCE HORSFALL

Each, crown 8vo, 60 cents, *net*. Postpaid.

These books are made up of a series of highly entertaining chapters dealing with sights, sounds, and experiences of the various seasons. Abstract and didactic discussions are avoided. Because of the personal, intimate touch with the reader throughout the books, and the numerous episodes revealing the author's sincere enjoyment of nature, boys and girls will read and reread these books with increasing delight and be much the richer for reading them.

"To entertain children with wonder stories," says a reviewer of *The Fall of the Year*, the first book in this Series to be published, "is not so commendable nor so exacting as to fascinate children with the facts of life. This larger task has been achieved brilliantly by Dallas Lore Sharp in his Nature Series. His observations are clear-eyed. His love of this wonderful world, intense though it be, does not befuddle his common sense. His conclusions are reasonable. Moreover, his sincere delight in everything shines through his words. He is irresistible."

HOUGHTON MIFFLIN COMPANY

BOSTON   NEW YORK   CHICAGO

DRAMATIC READERS

hildren's Classics in Dramatic Form. By AUGUSTA STEVENSON, formerly Teacher in the Indianapolis Public Schools.
Book One. 116 pages. Illustrated. 30 cents, *net*.
Book Two. 128 pages. Illustrated. 35 cents, *net*.
Book Three. 181 pages. Illustrated. 40 cents, *net*.
Book Four. 211 pages. Illustrated. 50 cents, *net*.
Book Five. *In preparation*.

MEMORIZING

Three Years with the Poets. Poems, selected and edited by BERTHA HAZARD. 247 pages, 50 cents, *net*.

Melodies of English Verse. By LEWIS KENNEDY MORSE. 184 pages, 80 cents, *net*.

MUSIC

The Riverside Graded Song Book for Elementary Schools. Edited by W. M. LAWRENCE, Principal of the W. H. Ray School, Chicago, Illinois.
Part One, for Primary and Intermediate Grades. 168 pages, boards, 40 cents, *net*.
Part Two, for Grammar Grades. 168 pages, boards, 40 cents, *net*.

The Riverside Song Book. Containing one hundred and twenty classic American Poems set to Standard Music. Selected and arranged by W. M. LAWRENCE and O. BLACKMAN, formerly Supervisor of Vocal Music in the Public Schools of Chicago. Paper, 30 cents, *net*; boards, 40 cents, *net*. 174 pages. *Riverside Literature Series*, Extra Number L.

Send for descriptive circulars

HOUGHTON MIFFLIN COMPANY
BOSTON NEW YORK CHICAGO

THE WOODS HUTCHINSON HEALTH SERIES

BY WOODS HUTCHINSON, M.D.

An ideal course in physiology and hygiene for elementary schools by a writer of international reputation as physician, teacher, and author.

BOOK ONE. THE CHILD'S DAY

For Grades III, IV or V. 40 cents, net. Postpaid.

A series of simple, practical, and interesting health-talks, giving the various experiences of a typical day and showing the child how he may build a strong, vigorous body and thereby immeasurably increase his happiness and usefulness.

BOOK TWO. A HANDBOOK OF HEALTH

For Grades VI, VII, VIII. 65 cents, net. Postpaid.

An authoritative and fully equipped textbook giving practical information regarding the body machinery and the promotion of health in the individual and in the community. It brings to the pupil in simple language the best information and advice of the medical profession of to-day.

HOUGHTON MIFFLIN COMPANY
BOSTON   NEW YORK   CHICAGO

LITERATURE TEXTS

American Classics. With suggestions for study, etc. 438 pages, 75 cents, *net*.

American and English Classics. For Grammar Grades. With explanatory notes, etc. 330 pages. 55 cents, *net*.

American Poems. Edited by H. E. SCUDDER. 453 pages, $1.00, *net*.

American Prose. Edited by H. E. SCUDDER. 414 pages, $1.00, *net*.

Literary Masterpieces. With explanatory notes, etc. 433 pages, 80 cents, *net*.

Masterpieces of American Literature. Edited by H. E. SCUDDER. With explanatory notes, etc. 504 pages, $1.00, *net*.

Masterpieces of British Literature. Edited by H. E. SCUDDER. With explanatory notes, etc. 480 pages, $1.00, *net*.

An American Anthology. Edited by E. C. STEDMAN. 878 pages. *Student's Edition.* $2.00, *net*.

A Victorian Anthology. Edited by E. C. STEDMAN. 744 pages. *Student's Edition.* $1.75, *net*.

The Chief American Poets. Edited by C. H. PAGE, Professor of English Literature in Northwestern University. 713 pages, $1.75, *net*.

Selections from the Riverside Literature Series. For Fifth Grade Reading. (In preparation.)

Selections from the Riverside Literature Series. For Sixth Grade Reading. With explanatory notes. 222 pages. 40 cents, *net*.

Selections from the Riverside Literature Series. For Seventh Grade Reading. With explanatory notes. 256 pages. 40 cents, *net*.

Selections from the Riverside Literature Series. For Eighth Grade Reading. With explanatory notes. 256 pages. 40 cents, *net*.

Riverside Literature Series. 223 volumes, with introductions, notes, biographical sketches, and illustrations. 170 volumes list at 15 cents, paper, or 25 cents, cloth, *net*.

Modern Classics. 34 volumes, pocket size, without notes. The uniform price is 40 cents, *net*.

Rolfe's Students' Series. 11 volumes of poems by Scott, Tennyson, Byron and Morris. Edited by W. J. ROLFE. Price to teachers, 53 cents, each, *net*.

HOUGHTON MIFFLIN COMPANY
BOSTON   NEW YORK   CHICAGO

"A STEP FORWARD IN READING"

THE RIVERSIDE READERS

EDITED BY
JAMES H. VAN SICKLE
Superintendent of Schools, Springfield, Mass.

AND
WILHELMINA SEEGMILLER
Late Director of Art, Indianapolis. Formerly Principal of the Wealthy Avenue Public School, Grand Rapids, Mich.

ASSISTED BY
FRANCES JENKINS
Supervisor of Elementary Grades, Decatur, Ill.

ILLUSTRATED BY
RUTH MARY HALLOCK   **CLARA E. ATWOOD**
MAGINEL WRIGHT ENRIGHT   **E. BOYD SMITH**
HOWARD PYLE, and other notable artists

FRESH MATERIAL
These Readers contain an unusually large amount of *fresh copyrighted material* taken from the world's best literature for children.

LATEST TEACHING METHODS
They represent the latest developments in the methods of teaching reading, the kind of teaching that will be found in the best schools of to-day.

ARTISTIC MAKE-UP
Artistically the books will set a new standard in text-book making. The colored illustrations of the primary books are particularly attractive.

MECHANICAL FEATURES
The paper used in the books, the type for each grade, and the dimensions and arrangement of the type page were all determined by careful experimenting, in order to safeguard the eyesight of children.

Send for complete illustrated circular describing the unique plan of this series

PRICES

Primer . . . . 30 cents *net*.	Fourth Reader	55 cents, *net*.
First Reader . . . . . 35 cents *net*.	Fifth Reader	55 cents, *net*.
Second Reader . . . . 40 cents *net*.	Sixth Reader	55 cents, *net*.
Third Reader . . . . . 50 cents *net*.	Seventh Reader . . .	55 cents, *net*.
	Eighth Reader, 60 cents, *net*.	

HOUGHTON MIFFLIN COMPANY
BOSTON   NEW YORK   CHICAGO

SUPPLEMENTARY READING

AUSTIN, MARY
    The Basket Woman. Indian Stories. *School Edition.* 220 pages, illustrated, 60 cents, *net*.

BROWN, ABBIE FARWELL
    The Book of Saints and Friendly Beasts. Animal Stories. Illustrated by Fanny Y. Cory. *School Edition.* 226 pages, 50 cents, *net*.

    In the Days of Giants. Norse Stories. Illustrated by E. Boyd Smith. *School Edition.* 259 pages, 50 cents, *net. Riverside Literature Series*, No. W.

ELIOT, SAMUEL (editor)
    Poetry for Children. Illustrated. 327 pages, 80 cents, *net*.

FIRTH, ABRAHAM (editor)
    Voices for the Speechless. Poems about animals and birds. 367 pages, $1.00.

HOLBROOK, FLORENCE
    Northland Heroes. Linen, 113 pages. Illustrated, 35 cents, *net. R. L. S.*, No. J.

LODGE, HENRY CABOT (editor)
    Ballads and Lyrics. 394 pages, $1.00, *net*.

MABIE, HAMILTON WRIGHT (editor)
    Heroes Every Child Should Know. *School Edition.* Illustrated. 288 pages, 40 cents, *net*.

RIVERSIDE ART SERIES
    Twelve volumes, edited by Estelle M. Hurll. Each volume contains about 96 pages, 16 full-page reproductions of characteristic Pictures with Interpretative Text, Introduction, and Pronouncing Vocabulary. Each, *School Edition*, 50 cents, *net*.

SHERMAN, FRANK DEMPSTER
    Little-Folk Lyrics. 140 pages. Illustrated. *School Edition.* 60 cents, *net*.

TAPPAN, EVA MARCH
    Old Ballads in Prose. Illustrated by Fanny Y. Cory. 164 pages. *School Edition.* 40 cents, *net*.

Send for descriptive circulars

HOUGHTON MIFFLIN COMPANY
BOSTON   NEW YORK   CHICAGO

ENGLISH LITERATURE

A Short History of England's Literature. By EVA MARCH TAPPAN, formerly of the English Department, English High School, Worcester, Mass., author of *England's Story, Our Country's Story,* etc. 253 pages, 85 cents, *net.*

A Student's History of English Literature. By William E. Simonds, Professor of English Literature in Knox College. 483 pages. $1.25, *net.*

Lives of Great English Writers. From Chaucer to Browning. By W. S. HINCHMAN, Instructor in English at the Groton School, and FRANCIS B. GUMMERE, Professor of English at Haverford College. 555 pages, $1.50, *net.*

AMERICAN LITERATURE

A Short History of England's and America's Literature. By EVA MARCH TAPPAN. 399 pages, $1.20, *net.*

A Short History of America's Literature. With Selections from Colonial and Revolutionary writers. By EVA MARCH TAPPAN. 246 pages, 80 cents, *net.*

A History of American Literature. By WILLIAM E. SIMONDS. 357 pages, $1.10, *net.*

A Primer of American Literature. By CHARLES F. RICHARDSON, Professor of English in Dartmouth College. 18mo, 140 pages, 35 cents, *net.*

Send for descriptive circulars

HOUGHTON MIFFLIN COMPANY
BOSTON   NEW YORK   CHICAGO

LaVergne, TN USA
22 July 2010
190439LV00002B/12/A